Algebra Workshop

Preparation for the Algebra Section of Standardized Tests

A self-teaching program to help improve mathematics skills that are tested on
- *Standardized tests* such as the Iowa, CAT, SRA, MAT and ERB.
- *College admission tests* such as the SAT and ACT.

by
Edward Williams

with
Elinor R. Ford, Ed.D.

Editorial Consultants

Kenneth Goldberg, Ph.D.
Professor of Mathematics Education
New York University
New York, New York

Sondra Reger
South Carroll High School
Sykesville, Maryland

Sadlier-Oxford
A Division of William H. Sadlier, Inc.
New York
Chicago
Los Angeles

Contents

Home Office:
7-9 Pine Street
New York, NY 10005

ISBN: 0-87105-471-X
23456789/98765432

What Is Algebra Workshop?

You have been preparing for Achievement and Aptitude Tests in all your mathematics courses. Most students need practice–study materials to review concepts found in the Algebra Section of these tests. ALGEBRA WORKSHOP is designed to help you prepare for all types of standardized tests.

The tests in this book are very much like the algebra section of an actual test. The *real* test and each *practice* test have the very same

- types of questions
- level of difficulty

Furthermore, there are special features in ALGEBRA WORKSHOP that will GET YOU READY for the actual test:

1. Diagnostic Tests with Sample Answer Sheets
These tests are designed to pinpoint students' weaknesses in the eight major areas of algebra.
- 40 questions on each test
- Answers keyed to Refresher Sections for quick reference to study materials

2. Algebra Refresher Sections with Problem Solving
The Algebra Refresher Sections provide a carefully developed review of concepts and skills in algebra.
- Integers
- Algebraic Expressions
- Factoring
- Equations
- Ratio and Proportion
- Probability
- Inequalities
- Problem Solving

3. Practice Tests
Practice Tests for each of the eight areas found in the Algebra Refresher Section.
- Integers Test
- Algebraic Expression Test
- Factoring Test
- Equations Test
- Ratio and Proportion Test
- Probability Test
- Inequalities Test
- Problem Solving Test
- Complete step-by-step solutions
- Answers keyed to Refresher Sections for quick reference to study materials
- *Error Analysis* for each test item

4. Two Sample SAT Algebra Tests
- 35 questions on each test
- Complete step-by-step solutions
- Answers keyed to Refresher Sections for quick reference to study materials
- Selected *Error Analysis* for each test

How the Algebra Workshop Works

The special features of the ALGEBRA WORKSHOP are
- clear, concise presentations of solutions
- selected error analysis for self-improvement

Example:

If $x = 2$, then $\dfrac{\sqrt{(x^2)^x + x^3}}{x} =$

(A) $\sqrt{6}$ (B) $2\sqrt{3}$ (C) $\frac{1}{2}\sqrt{14}$ (D) $\frac{1}{2}\sqrt{22}$ (E) 2

Solution:

(A) Substitute 2 for x and evaluate the expression.

$$\frac{\sqrt{(x^2)^x + x^3}}{x} = \frac{\sqrt{(2^2)^2 + 2^3}}{2}$$

$$= \frac{\sqrt{4^2 + 2^3}}{2} = \frac{\sqrt{16 + 8}}{2} = \frac{\sqrt{24}}{2}$$

$$= \frac{\sqrt{4 \cdot 6}}{2} = \frac{2\sqrt{6}}{2}$$

$$= \frac{\overset{1}{\cancel{2}}\sqrt{6}}{\underset{1}{\cancel{2}}} = \sqrt{6}$$

Error Analysis:

If your choice was

(B), you divided $\sqrt{24}$ by 2. Thus, $\frac{\sqrt{24}}{2} \neq \sqrt{12} = 2\sqrt{3}$.

(C), you computed 4^2 as 8 and 2^3 as 6.

(D), you computed 2^3 as 6.

(E), you computed 4^2 as 8.

- For additional help, see Algebra Refresher Section 2.1 beginning on page 23.

- For further help, see Algebraic Expressions Test on page 82.

- For further preparation in mathematics for standardized tests, use the other books in this series.

Arithmetic Workshop

Geometry Workshop

Mathematics Workshop — Preparation for the Mathematics Section of the SAT

Types of Multiple-Choice Questions

There are two types of multiple-choice questions used in the mathematics section of standardized tests: the standard multiple-choice questions and quantitative comparison questions.

The standard multiple-choice questions offer 5 choices as solutions, but only 4 choices are given in the quantitative comparison questions.

● **Standard Multiple-Choice Questions**
These questions are familiar to most students. A problem is presented with 5 possible answer choices and you are to solve the problem and select the best of the choices given. Then you are to blacken in the space on the answer sheet corresponding to your answer choice.

EXAMPLE: If $a = 2 \cdot 3 \cdot 5$ and $b = 2 \cdot 3$, then $a + b$ is equal to the product of 6 and

(A) 5   (B) 6   (C) 1   (D) -6 (E) -5

Since $a = 2 \cdot 3 \cdot 5$ and $b = 2 \cdot 3$,

then $a = 30$ and $b = 6$.
So $a + b = 6 \cdot n$ (Missing factor)
$$30 + 6 = 6n$$
$$36 = 6n$$
$$6 = n$$

Answer B is the best choice, so blacken circle B on the answer sheet. Ⓐ ● Ⓒ Ⓓ Ⓔ

● **Quantitative Comparison Questions**
You may not be as familiar with this type of problem as you are with standard multiple-choice questions. Quantitative comparison questions require the use of estimation skills and an understanding of inequalities. Less computation and reading are needed to answer them, but critical thinking is essential. In order to improve your skills, be sure you understand the directions and practice solving as many quantitative comparison questions as possible.

To solve a quantitative comparison problem, you compare the quantities in the two columns and decide whether one quantity is greater than the other, whether the two quantities are equal, or whether the comparison cannot be determined from the information given.

5

The directions and notes are reprinted here exactly as they will appear on the actual Scholastic Aptitude Test.

EXAMPLE:

Column A	Column B
$x * y$ is defined as $\dfrac{x + y}{x}$	
$6 * 3$	$4 * 2$

If
then

$$x * y = \frac{x + y}{x},$$
$$6 * 3 = \frac{6 + 3}{6} = \frac{9}{6} \text{ or } \frac{3}{2}$$
$$4 * 2 = \frac{4 + 2}{4} = \frac{6}{4} \text{ or } \frac{3}{2}$$

Since $6 * 3$ and $4 * 2$ are equal, space C is blackened.

<u>Answers:</u>   Ⓐ Ⓑ ● Ⓓ Ⓔ

Since these questions have four answer choices: A, B, C, and D, you must be careful not to mark E as an answer.

If additional information or diagrams are needed, it will appear above the quantities to be compared.

*Directions reprinted with permission of Educational Testing Service, the copyright owner. From *Taking the SAT, 1986-87*; College Entrance Examination Board, New York. This booklet describes the tests, gives tips on test-taking strategies, and explains the different kinds of questions. The booklet may be obtained on request by writing to the College Board ATP, CN 6200, Princeton, NJ 08541-6200

Test-Taking Tips
Preparing for the Test

> To make sure you are prepared for the test, you should
> 1. be familiar with its organization
> 2. know the types of questions that will appear on it
> 3. know what is expected of you on the test day

1. Be Familiar with its Organization

- Is there more than one part to the test?
- Is there a time limit for the entire test?
- Is there a time limit for each part?
- How many questions are there in all?
- Do I need special tools for the test?
- Can a calculator be used during the test?
- Will there be a separate answer sheet?
- How many choices for answers will there be?
- How do I mark my answer on the answer sheet?
- Will I gain or lose points if I omit an answer?
- Is there a penalty for guessing an answer?

2. Know the Types of Questions

- Will there be standard multiple-choice questions?
- Will there be quantitative comparison questions?
- Will there be another type of question on the test with which I am not familiar?
- Are sample tests available with which I can practice?

Read and study the information on *Types of Multiple-Choice Questions* found on pp. 5-6, in this book.

3. What is Expected on the Test Day

- Do I know the location of the testing center?
- Do I know the time of the examination?
- How much time will I need to travel to the testing center?
- Did I bring the tools, if any, that are needed for the test?
- Do I need an admissions ticket?
- Do I need acceptable identification?
- Did I get a good night's sleep?
- Do I feel well prepared to take the test?

During the Test

To make sure you score as high as you can on the test, you should
1. read the question carefully
2. search out groups of questions of the same type
3. estimate before you actually complete the answer
4. use an *educated* guess

1. Read the Question Carefully
- Do I understand the directions for the question?
- Do I know what is being asked in the question?
- Have I reread the question to be sure that I have answered it?
- Is my answer reasonable?

2. Group Questions of the Same Type
- Did I look for the questions I know how to do and complete these first?
- Did I mark off with an "X" through the number of the question, those questions which I know how to do and have completed.
- Did I mark off with an "/" through the number of the question, those questions of which I am not sure but have completed?
- Did I leave unmarked, the numbers of the questions I did not answer and must return to later?

3. Estimate the Answer
- Is my computed answer reasonable when compared to my estimated answer?
- If my computed answer and estimated answer do not correspond, do I know which is correct?
- Is there an alternative method I can use to solve the problem?

4. Use an *Educated* Guess
- Can I estimate the answer without doing the actual computation?
- Can I eliminate as definitely wrong one or more choices for the answer?
- Can I, fairly accurately, choose the correct answer from the remaining choices?

Part One

Two Diagnostic Tests

This section contains two Diagnostic Tests designed to help pinpoint weaknesses in eight areas of algebra. These areas are

- Integers
- Algebraic Expressions
- Factoring
- Equations
- Ratio and Proportion
- Probability
- Inequalities
- Problem Solving

Use the Answer Sheet that precedes each test to record your answers. The Answer Sheet for Test 1 is found on page 10 and the Answer Sheet for Test 2 is found on page 16. After you have completed each test, you can check your answers using the Answer Key on page 22.

If you need additional help, each answer is referenced (in parentheses) to the appropriate Algebra Refresher Section.

Answer Sheet

Diagnostic Test 1

INTEGERS

1. Ⓐ ● Ⓒ Ⓓ
2. Ⓐ Ⓑ ● Ⓓ
3. Ⓐ Ⓑ Ⓒ ●
4. ● Ⓑ Ⓒ Ⓓ
5. Ⓐ Ⓑ Ⓒ ●

ALGEBRAIC EXPRESSIONS

6. Ⓐ ● Ⓒ Ⓓ
7. Ⓐ Ⓑ Ⓒ Ⓓ
8. Ⓐ Ⓑ ● Ⓓ
9. ● Ⓑ Ⓒ Ⓓ
10. Ⓐ Ⓑ Ⓒ ●

FACTORING

11. ● Ⓑ Ⓒ Ⓓ
12. Ⓐ Ⓑ ● Ⓓ
13. Ⓐ Ⓑ ● Ⓓ
14. Ⓐ Ⓑ ● Ⓓ
15. ● Ⓑ Ⓒ Ⓓ

EQUATIONS

16. ● Ⓑ Ⓒ Ⓓ
17. ● Ⓑ Ⓒ Ⓓ
18. Ⓐ Ⓑ ● Ⓓ
19. Ⓐ ● Ⓒ Ⓓ
20. ● Ⓑ ● Ⓓ

RATIO AND PROPORTION

21. ● Ⓑ Ⓒ Ⓓ
22. Ⓐ ● Ⓒ Ⓓ
23. ● Ⓑ Ⓒ Ⓓ
24. Ⓐ ● Ⓒ Ⓓ
25. Ⓐ Ⓑ ● Ⓓ

PROBABILITY

26. Ⓐ Ⓑ ● Ⓓ
27. Ⓐ ● Ⓒ Ⓓ
28. Ⓐ Ⓑ Ⓒ Ⓓ
29. Ⓐ Ⓑ Ⓒ Ⓓ
30. Ⓐ Ⓑ Ⓒ Ⓓ

INEQUALITIES

31. Ⓐ Ⓑ Ⓒ Ⓓ
32. Ⓐ Ⓑ Ⓒ Ⓓ
33. Ⓐ Ⓑ Ⓒ Ⓓ
34. Ⓐ Ⓑ Ⓒ Ⓓ
35. Ⓐ Ⓑ Ⓒ Ⓓ

PROBLEM SOLVING

36. Ⓐ Ⓑ Ⓒ Ⓓ
37. Ⓐ Ⓑ Ⓒ Ⓓ
38. Ⓐ Ⓑ Ⓒ Ⓓ
39. Ⓐ Ⓑ Ⓒ Ⓓ
40. Ⓐ Ⓑ Ⓒ Ⓓ

Diagnostic Test 1

Directions:
Solve each problem in this diagnostic test. Use any available space on the page for scratchwork. Then decide which is the best of the choices given and either darken the corresponding space on the Answer Sheet on page 10 or circle your answer from among the choices provided.

INTEGERS

1. $(+9) + (-3) =$
   (A) -12 (B) $+6$ (C) $+12$ (D) -6

2. $(-12) \div (-6) =$
   (A) -2 (B) -6 (C) $+2$ (D) -6

3. $(-2)^5 =$
   (A) 2^5 (B) -10 (C) $+10$ (D) -2^5

4. $- \frac{-1}{3} =$
   (A) $\frac{1}{3}$ (B) $-\frac{1}{3}$ (C) $-\frac{1}{3}$ (D) $-\frac{1}{3}$

5. $(-\frac{1}{3})(-\frac{1}{2})(-3)(-2) =$
   (A) -1 (B) $+1$ (C) $5\frac{5}{6}$ (D) 30

ALGEBRAIC EXPRESSIONS

6. $3a - (2a - b) =$
   (A) $5a - b$ (B) $a + b$ (C) $5a + b$ (D) $a - b$

7. $\left(\frac{3xy^2}{5ab^3}\right)\left(\frac{10a^2b}{xy^3}\right) =$
   (A) $\frac{6ax}{b^2y}$ (B) $\frac{6ay}{b^2}$ (C) $\frac{6a}{b^2y}$ (D) $\frac{5a}{b^2y}$

8. If $x = 4$, then $\sqrt{\frac{(x-1)^2 + 2^x}{x}} =$
   (A) $1\frac{1}{4}$ (B) $\sqrt{6}$ (C) $2\frac{1}{2}$ (D) $6\frac{1}{4}$

9. $3x + (2 - x)(x + 4) =$
   (A) $8 - 5x - x^2$ (B) $8 + x - x^2$
   (C) $x^2 + x - 8$ (D) $x^2 + x + 8$

11

10. A number, n, is divided by 4. Three less than the result would be represented by

(A) $\frac{4}{n} - 3$ (B) $3 - \frac{n}{4}$ (C) $\frac{1}{n}$ (D) $\frac{n}{4} - 3$

FACTORING

11. Factor $16a^2 - b^4$.

(A) $(4a - b^2)(4a + b^2)$
(B) $(8a - b^2)(8a + b^2)$
(C) $(8a - b^2)(2a + b^2)$
(D) $(2a - b^2)(8a + b^2)$

12. What is the greatest common factor of the expression $4x^2 + 32x^3y$?

(A) 4 (B) x (C) $4x^2$ (D) $4x^3$

13. Factor $a^2 - 7a + 6$.

(A) $(a - 1)(a + 6)$
(B) $(a + 1)(a + 6)$
(C) $(a - 1)(a - 6)$
(D) $(a + 1)(a - 6)$

14. Factor $2x^2 - 3x - 2$.

(A) $(2x - 1)(x + 2)$
(B) $(2x + 1)(x - 2)$
(C) $(2x - 2)(x + 1)$
(D) $(2x - 1)(x - 2)$

15. Factor $a^4 - b^4$ completely.

(A) $(a^2 + b^2)(a^2 - b^2)$
(B) $(a^2 - b^2)(a^2 - b^2)$
(C) $(a + b)^2(a - b)^2$
(D) $(a^2 + b^2)(a - b)(a + b)$

EQUATIONS

16. If $x = 2y - 3$ and $y = \frac{3}{2}$, then $x =$

(A) 0 (B) 1 (C) 2 (D) 6

17. Solve the equation $3x - 4 = 5x + 8$.

(A) -6 (B) $-1\frac{1}{2}$ (C) $1\frac{1}{2}$ (D) 6

18. If $x + y = 8$ and $3y = 12$, then $x =$

(A) -4 (B) -1 (C) 4 (D) 5

19. Solve the quadratic equation $x^2 - 5x + 6 = 0$.

(A) $x = -3, x = 2$
(B) $x = 3, x = 2$
(C) $x = 3, x = -2$
(D) $x = -3, x = -2$

20. Solve the equation $y - x = 2x + 3$ for x in terms of y.

(A) $3y - 3$
(B) $\frac{y - 3}{3}$
(C) $\frac{y}{3} - 3$
(D) $y - 3$

RATIO AND PROPORTION

21. The ratio which represents the same ratio as $6:5$ is

(A) 12:10   (B) 10:12   (C) 13:15   (D) 35:25

22. If $a:b = 4:5$, then $b:a$ is equal to

(A) 5:1   (B) 5:4   (C) 5:-4   (D) 9:1

23. If z is to 6 as 10 is to 15, then $z =$

(A) 4
(B) 6
(C) 8
(D) 9

24. If a is to b as c is to d, then

(A) $ac = bd$ (B) $a:c = d:b$
(C) $b:a = c:d$ (D) $ad = bc$

25. If there are 100 centimeters in a meter, how many centimeters are there in 1.3 meters?

(A) 0.13   (B) 13   (C) 130   (D) 1300

PROBABILITY

26. In how many ways can 2 offices be filled if there are 3 candidates for governor and 4 candidates for mayor?

(A) 1   (B) 7
(C) 12   (D) 34

27. A student has a choice of 5 music classes and 4 art classes. In how many ways can she choose one music and one art class?

(A) 9   (B) 20
(C) 24   (D) 54

28. A man wants a sandwich and a drink for lunch. If a restaurant has 6 choices of sandwiches and 4 choices of drinks, how many different ways can he order his lunch?

(A) 2   (B) 10   (C) 24   (D) 64

29. A spinner has 6 numbers on its face. If 2 numbers are needed to win a game, how many possible winning combinations are there?

(A) 12   (B) 24   (C) 30   (D) 36

30. A box contains 3 black balls and 2 white balls. If Jane is blindfolded, what is the chance that Jane will pick a black ball?

(A) $\frac{3}{5}$ (B) $\frac{2}{5}$ (C) $\frac{3}{2}$ (D) $\frac{2}{3}$

INEQUALITIES

31. If $2 - y < 2y + 2$, then

(A) $y = 0$
(B) $y > 0$
(C) $y < 0$
(D) $y > -4$

32. If $a^2 + a > 1$, then which of the following is always true?

(A) $a > 1$
(B) $a > -1$
(C) $a > \frac{1}{2}$
(D) $a > 0$

33. If $x > y$ and $y > z$, then

(A) $xy > yz$ (B) $x > z$
(C) $x + y > z$ (D) $xyz > 0$

34. If $1 - 2x < 0$, then

(A) $x < \frac{1}{2}$ (B) $x < 1$
(C) $x > \frac{1}{2}$ (D) $x > 1$

35. If $x > y$, then which of the following is always false?

(A) $xy > 0$
(B) $x^2 > y^2$
(C) $x - y < 0$
(D) $5x < 3y$

PROBLEM SOLVING

36. One more than 4 times 3 less than some number is 9. What is the number?

(A) 20
(B) 5
(C) $2\frac{3}{4}$
(D) $4\frac{1}{4}$

37. Find the largest of 3 consecutive even integers such that the largest is 3 times the smallest.

(A) 6
(B) 12
(C) 8
(D) 20

38. A freight train travels 5 hours moving at 40 miles per hour. How long would the trip take in a 100 mile per hour passenger train?

(A) $\frac{1}{2}$ hour
(B) 1 hour
(C) 2 hours
(D) 4 hours

39. A chemist has 3 quarts of a 20% acid solution. He wants to add a 6% acid solution so as to obtain a 12% acid solution. How many quarts of the 6% solution must be used?

(A) 2
(B) 4
(C) 6
(D) 8

40. Jenny has the same number of 14¢ stamps as 17¢ stamps. She also has as many 22¢ stamps as the number of 14¢ and 17¢ stamps combined. If the total value of all the stamps is $2K$ dollars, how many 22¢ stamps does she have?

(A) $\frac{8}{3}K$

(B) $\frac{16}{3}K$

(C) $\frac{40}{7}K$

(D) $\frac{200}{53}K$

Answer Sheet

Diagnostic Test 2

INTEGERS

1. Ⓐ Ⓑ Ⓒ Ⓓ
2. Ⓐ Ⓑ Ⓒ Ⓓ
3. Ⓐ Ⓑ Ⓒ Ⓓ
4. Ⓐ Ⓑ Ⓒ Ⓓ
5. Ⓐ Ⓑ Ⓒ Ⓓ

ALGEBRAIC EXPRESSIONS

6. Ⓐ Ⓑ Ⓒ Ⓓ
7. Ⓐ Ⓑ Ⓒ Ⓓ
8. Ⓐ Ⓑ Ⓒ Ⓓ
9. Ⓐ Ⓑ Ⓒ Ⓓ
10. Ⓐ Ⓑ Ⓒ Ⓓ

FACTORING

11. Ⓐ Ⓑ Ⓒ Ⓓ
12. Ⓐ Ⓑ Ⓒ Ⓓ
13. Ⓐ Ⓑ Ⓒ Ⓓ
14. Ⓐ Ⓑ Ⓒ Ⓓ
15. Ⓐ Ⓑ Ⓒ Ⓓ

EQUATIONS

16. Ⓐ Ⓑ Ⓒ Ⓓ
17. Ⓐ Ⓑ Ⓒ Ⓓ
18. Ⓐ Ⓑ Ⓒ Ⓓ
19. Ⓐ Ⓑ Ⓒ Ⓓ
20. Ⓐ Ⓑ Ⓒ Ⓓ

RATIO AND PROPORTION

21. Ⓐ Ⓑ Ⓒ Ⓓ
22. Ⓐ Ⓑ Ⓒ Ⓓ
23. Ⓐ Ⓑ Ⓒ Ⓓ
24. Ⓐ Ⓑ Ⓒ Ⓓ
25. Ⓐ Ⓑ Ⓒ Ⓓ

PROBABILITY

26. Ⓐ Ⓑ Ⓒ Ⓓ
27. Ⓐ Ⓑ Ⓒ Ⓓ
28. Ⓐ Ⓑ Ⓒ Ⓓ
29. Ⓐ Ⓑ Ⓒ Ⓓ
30. Ⓐ Ⓑ Ⓒ Ⓓ

INEQUALITIES

31. Ⓐ Ⓑ Ⓒ Ⓓ
32. Ⓐ Ⓑ Ⓒ Ⓓ
33. Ⓐ Ⓑ Ⓒ Ⓓ
34. Ⓐ Ⓑ Ⓒ Ⓓ
35. Ⓐ Ⓑ Ⓒ Ⓓ

PROBLEM SOLVING

36. Ⓐ Ⓑ Ⓒ Ⓓ
37. Ⓐ Ⓑ Ⓒ Ⓓ
38. Ⓐ Ⓑ Ⓒ Ⓓ
39. Ⓐ Ⓑ Ⓒ Ⓓ
40. Ⓐ Ⓑ Ⓒ Ⓓ

Diagnostic Test 2

INTEGERS

1. $(-2) - (-2) + (+2) =$

   (A) -2 (B) 2 (C) 4 (D) 6

2. $(-2) - (-8) =$

   (A) -10 (B) -6 (C) 6 (D) 16

3. $\left(-\frac{5}{6}\right) \div \left(-\frac{1}{2}\right) =$

   (A) $\frac{-5}{3}$ (B) $-\frac{5}{3}$ (C) $-\frac{-5}{3}$ (D) $\frac{5}{3}$

4. $(+15) + (-12) =$

   (A) -27
   (B) -3
   (C) $+3$
   (D) $+27$

5. $(-1)(-2)(-3)(+4) =$

   (A) -24 (B) -2 (C) 24 (D) 36

ALGEBRAIC EXPRESSIONS

6. $5c^3 + 2d^3 - 3c^3 =$

   (A) $2c^6 - 2d^3$ (B) $2(c^3 + d^3)$
   (C) $4c^3d^3$ (D) $2c^3 + d^3$

7. $4x + (2y - x) =$

   (A) $5x + 2y$ (B) $2y - 3x$
   (C) $3x + 2y$ (D) $5xy$

8. Combine $\frac{a}{2} + \frac{1}{a}$

   (A) $\frac{a^2 + 2}{2a}$ (B) $\frac{a^2 + 3}{2a}$

   (C) $\frac{a + 1}{2a}$ (D) $\frac{a^2 + 2}{a}$

9. If $x = 2$ and $y = -1$, then $-3y - 2x =$

(A) −7   (B) −1   (C) 0   (D) 7

10. $(x + 1)(3x - 2) - 4(x - 1) =$

(A) $3x^2 - 3x - 2$
(B) $3x^2 - 3x + 2$
(C) $3x^2 - 5x - 2$
(D) $3x^2 - 3x - 6$

FACTORING

11. Factor $7xy - x^2y - 14x^3y$.

(A) $7xy (1 - x - 2x^2)$
(B) $7x (y - xy - 2x^2y)$
(C) $xy (7 - x - 2x^2)$
(D) $xy (7 - x - 14x^2)$

12. Which of the following is a perfect square?

(A) $8x^4$ (B) a^4b^2 (C) y^5 (D) xy

13. Factor $3x^2 + 4x - 15$.

(A) $(3x + 5)(x - 3)$
(B) $(x + 3)(3x + 5)$
(C) $(3x - 5)(x - 3)$
(D) $(x + 3)(3x - 5)$

14. Factor $100m^4 - n^2$.

(A) $(10m^2 + n)(10m^2 - n)$
(B) $(50m^2 - n)(50m^2 - n)$
(C) $(25m^2 + n)(4m^2 - n)$
(D) $(25m^2 - n)(4m^2 + n)$

15. Factor $8a^3 - 8ab^2$ completely.

(A) $a(8a + b)(a - b)$
(B) $8ab(a^2 - b)$
(C) $a(8a^2 - 8b^2)$
(D) $8a(a + b)(a - b)$

EQUATIONS

16. If $3x = 2y$, then

(A) $3x + 4 = 2y - 4$ (B) $3x - 2y = 0$
(C) $3x + 2y = 0$ (D) $x = y$

17. In the equation $3a - 4 = 5a + 8$, $a =$

(A) -6
(B) $-\frac{5}{2}$
(C) 2
(D) 6

18. Find the solutions to the equation $z^2 - 3z - 40 = 0$.

(A) $z = 8, z = 5$
(B) $z = -8, z = 5$
(C) $z = 8, z = -5$
(D) $z = -8, z = -5$

19. If $x = y + 5$ and $2x + y = 7$, then $y =$

(A) -3
(B) -1
(C) 0
(D) 3

20. If $2x = 3 - (x - 3)$, then $5x =$

(A) 0
(B) 2
(C) 10
(D) 30

RATIO AND PROPORTION

21. The ratio that is equivalent to $16:6$ is

(A) $3:8$　　(B) $3:22$　　(C) $4:1$　　(D) $8:3$

22. If a is to 12 as 2 is to 3, then $a =$

(A) 6 　　　　　　(B) 8
(C) 18 　　　　　(D) 24

23. The proportion that means the same as $xw = yz$ is

(A) $x:w = y:z$ 　　　(B) $x:w = z.y$
(C) $x:y = z:w$ 　　　(D) $x:y = w:z$

24. On a map 1 cm represents 60 km. Two cities, 150 km apart, would be separated on the map by

(A) 1 cm 　　　　　(B) 2 cm
(C) 2.5 cm 　　　　(D) 3 cm

25. If $\frac{4}{x} = \frac{x}{16}$, then x could equal

(A) 32 　　　　　(B) 4
(C) 8 　　　　　 (D) 32

PROBABILITY

26. Eight boys and 12 girls attend a party. How many different dancing pairs can be formed?

    (A) 4   (B) 20   (C) 80   (D) 96

27. A die is numbered from 1 to 6. What is the probability of a 5 landing face up on one toss of the die?

    (A) $\frac{1}{6}$ (B) $\frac{1}{5}$ (C) $\frac{1}{2}$ (D) 1

28. Three men and 2 women are ready to enter a room. If they enter the room in a random fashion, what is the chance that a man will enter the room first?

    (A) $\frac{3}{5}$ (B) $\frac{2}{5}$ (C) $\frac{3}{2}$ (D) $\frac{2}{3}$

29. In a selected group of singers a music teacher has 5 sopranos, 4 altos, 4 basses, and 2 tenors. How many quartets may be chosen from this group?

    (A) 15   (B)   48
    (C) $8\frac{1}{2}$ (D) 160

30. A room has 5 doors. In how many ways can a person enter the room and leave by any door?

    (A) 5   (B) 10   (C) 20   (D) 25

INEQUALITIES

31. A solution for the inequality $2x - 3 < 3$ could be

    (A) -3 (B) 3
    (C)   5   (D) 7

32. If $\frac{x}{2} > \frac{1}{2}$, then x could be

    (A) -1 (B) 0   (C) 1   (D) 2

33. If $x < y$, then which of the following is always true?

    (A) $xy > 0$ (B) $x^2 < y^2$
    (C) $x - y < 0$ (D) $3x < 2y$

34. If $\frac{1}{x} < \frac{1}{2}$, then x could be

    (A) -1 (B) 0   (C) 1   (D) 2

35. If $a > b$ and $c > d$, then which of the following is always true?

    (A) $ac > bd$ (B) $a + c > b + d$
    (C) $a \quad c > b \quad d$ (D) $\frac{a}{c} > \frac{b}{d}$

PROBLEM SOLVING

36. Which equation represents the following information:
If 25% of a number n is 80, find the number.

(A) $n = 0.25(80)$
(B) $0.25n = 80$
(C) $\frac{n}{0.25} = 80$
(D) $80n = 0.25$

37. Sue jogged for one hour moving at 8 miles per hour. How long would the same trip take if she walked at the rate of 4 miles per hour?

(A) 1 hour
(B) 2 hours
(C) 3 hours
(D) 4 hours

38. Two positive numbers are in the ratio of 5 to 13. If the difference between the two numbers is 48, then the larger number is

(A) 30
(B) 65
(C) 78
(D) 91

39. The cost of a high school ring is $45 for the large size and $35 for the regular size. The number of large-size rings sold is twice the number of the regular-size rings sold. If the total receipts from the sale is K dollars, how many regular-size rings were sold?

(A) $\frac{K}{125}$

(B) $\frac{K}{115}$

(C) $\frac{125}{K}$

(D) $125K$

40. The cost C, in cents, of x pounds of a product is given by the formula $C = kx + b$, where k and b are constants. If the cost of 3 pounds is $.84 and the cost of 7 pounds is $1.96, then $k =$

(A) 12
(B) 28
(C) 40
(D) It cannot be determined from the information given.

Answer Key
to Diagnostic Tests

Following each answer, there is a number or numbers in the form "*a.b*" in parentheses. This number refers to the Algebra Refresher Section (beginning on page 23). The first number "*a*" indicates the Math section:

1. Integers
2. Algebraic Expressions
3. Factoring
4. Equations

5. Ratio and Proportion
6. Probability
7. Inequalities
8. Problem Solving

The second number "*b*" indicates the part of the section that explains the rule or method used in solving the problem.

DIAGNOSTIC TEST 1

1. B (1.4, 1.3)
2. C (1.8, 1.3)
3. D (2.1, 1.6)
4. A (1.5)
5. B (1.6)
6. B (2.8, 2.7)
7. C (2.9, 2.10)
8. C (2.6, 2.1)
9. B (2.9, 2.8, 2.7)
10. D (2.3)
11. A (3.4, 2.1)
12. C (2.3)
13. C (3.5)
14. B (3.5)

15. D (3.4, 3.6)
16. A (4.2)
17. A (4.3)
18. C (4.2, 4.3)
19. B (4.4, 3.5)
20. B (4.5, 4.3)
21. A (5.1)
22. B (5.1)
23. A (5.4)
24. D (5.4, 5.3)
25. C (5.5, 5.4)
26. C (6.1)
27. B (6.1)
28. C (6.1)

29. D (6.1)
30. A (6.2)
31. B (7.4, 7.3)
32. A (7.4, 2.6)
33. B (7.2)
34. C (7.4, 7.3)
35. C (7.1, 2.6)
36. B (8.1, 4.3)
37. A (8.2, 4.3)
38. C (8.3, 4.3)
39. B (8.4)
40. B (8.5)

DIAGNOSTIC TEST 2

1. B (1.4, 1.5, 1.3)
2. C (1.5, 1.4)
3. D (1.8)
4. C (1.4)
5. A (1.6)
6. B (2.8, 2.7)
7. C (2.8, 2.7)
8. A (2.7)
9. B (2.6)
10. B (2.9, 2.8)
11. D (3.3)
12. B (2.1)
13. D (3.5)
14. A (3.4)

15. D (3.3, 3.6, 3.4)
16. B (4.2)
17. A (4.3, 4.2)
18. C (4.4, 3.5)
19. B (4.6, 4.2)
20. C (4.3)
21. D (5.1)
22. B (5.4)
23. C (5.4, 5.3)
24. C (5.5, 5.4)
25. C (5.4, 2.1)
26. D (6.1)
27. A (6.2)
28. A (6.2)

29. D (6.1)
30. D (6.1)
31. A (7.1, 7.4, 7.3)
32. D (7.4, 7.3)
33. C (7.3)
34. A (7.4, 7.3)
35. B (7.3)
36. B (2.3)
37. B (8.3, 4.3)
38. C (8.1, 4.3)
39. A (8.7, 2.3)
40. B (8.7, 2.3)

Part Two

Algebra Refresher Sections

The Algebra Refresher Sections provide a carefully developed review of concepts and skills in algebra. These sections contain definitions, illustrations, and examples designed to help you solve many different types of algebra questions which appear on actual standardized tests in Mathematics. Be sure you are familiar with and understand each of the illustrated methods and examples.

Algebra Refresher

Integers, Algebraic Expressions, Factoring, Equations, Ratio and Proportion, Probability, Inequalities, and Problem Solving

INTEGERS

Integers are any of the numbers
$$\cdots, -2, -1, 0, 1, 2, \cdots.$$
The *positive integers* (or natural numbers) are 1, 2, 3, $\cdots$ and the *negative integers* are $-1, -2, -3, \cdots$.

1.1   Number Line

A *number line* is a line on which points are associated with numbers in a one-to-one correspondence. The set of integers can be pictured on a number line.

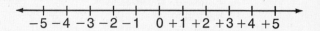

The negative integers are those numbers less than 0 and the positive integers are those numbers greater than 0. If the sign of the number is omitted, the number is understood to be positive. Thus, $9 = +9$.

1.2   Comparing and Ordering Integers

The number line helps us to see how integers can be compared. Given two integers, the greater integer is associated with a point on the number line which is the right of the point associated with the other integer.

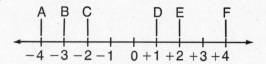

Point F is to the right of point D, point E is to the right of point B, and point C is to the right of point A.

Therefore, $+4 > +1$, $+2 > -3$, and $-2 > -4$.

On a vertical number line, any integer is greater than the integers below it, but less than those above it.

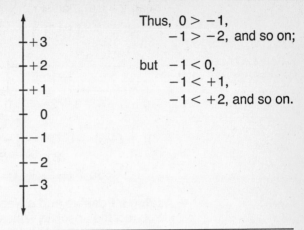

Thus, $0 > -1$,
$-1 > -2$, and so on;
but $-1 < 0$,
$-1 < +1$,
$-1 < +2$, and so on.

1.3 Absolute Value

The *absolute value* of a number, whether the number is positive or negative, is always positive. The absolute value of an integer can be shown on the number line as its distance from 0.

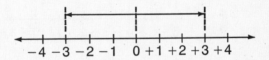

The absolute value of 3 or -3 is 3 since each number is 3 units from 0. The absolute value of 0 is 0.

The symbol for the absolute value of a number is a vertical bar on each side of the number:

$$|+3| = 3 \qquad |-3| = 3 \qquad |0| = 0$$

1.4 Adding Integers

- **Adding Two Positive Integers**
  - Add the absolute values.
  - Keep the common sign.

EXAMPLE: Add $(+1)$ and $(+4)$.

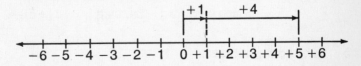

$(+1) + (+4) \rightarrow |+1| + |+4| =$
$\qquad\qquad\qquad 1 \;+\; 4 \;= 5$
So, $(+1) + (+4) = +5.$

25

● Adding Two Negative Integers
- Add the absolute values.
- Keep the common sign.

EXAMPLE: Add $(-2) + (-3)$.

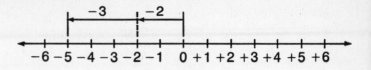

$(-2) + (-3) \rightarrow |-2| + |-3| =$
$$2 + 3 = 5$$
So, $(-2) + (-3) = -5$.

● Adding a Positive and a Negative Integer
- Subtract the absolute values.
- Give this difference the sign of the integer with the greater absolute value.

EXAMPLE: Add $(-6) + (+2)$.

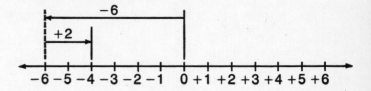

$(-6) + (+2) \rightarrow |-6| + |+2| =$
$$6 - 2 = 4$$
Since $|-6| > |+2|$, then $(-6) + (+2) = -4$.

EXAMPLE: Add $(+5) + (-3)$.

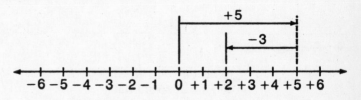

$(+5) + (-3) \rightarrow |+5| + |-3| =$
$$5 - 3 = 2$$
Since $|+5| > |-3|$, then $(+5) + (-3) = +2$

1.5   Subtracting Integers

- Change the sign of the subtrahend (the number to be subtracted).
- Follow the rules for adding integers.

EXAMPLES:
$$(+7) - (+3) = (+7) + (-3) = +4$$
$$(+7) - (-3) = (+7) + (+3) = +10$$
$$(-7) - (+3) = (-7) + (-3) = -10$$
$$(-7) - (-3) = (-7) + (+3) = -4$$

1.6 Multiplying Integers

There are two cases to consider:

1. When the factors have the same sign
- find the product of the absolute values of the factors.
- the sign of the product is positive.

EXAMPLES:
$$(+2) \times (+4) = +8 \qquad (-2) \times (-4) = +8$$

In place of the multiplication symbol, you can use an upraised dot or omit the sign completely.
For example: $(+2) \times (+4) = (+2) \cdot (+4) = (+2)(+4)$.

2. When the factors have different signs
- find the product of the absolute values of the factors.
- the sign of the product is negative.

EXAMPLES:
$$(-2) \times (+4) = -8 \qquad (+2) \times (-4) = -8$$

1.7 Properties of Addition and Multiplication of Integers

Property	Addition of Integers	Multiplication of Integers
Closure	If a and b are integers, then $a + b = c$ where c is an integer.	If a and b are integers, then $ab = c$ where c is an integer.
Commutative	If a and b are integers, then $a + b = b + a$.	If a and b are integers, then $ab = ba$.
Associative	If a, b, and c are integers, then $a + (b + c) = (a + b) + c$.	If a, b, and c are integers, then $a(bc) = (ab)c$.
Identity Element	If a is any integer, then $a + 0 = a$.	If a is any integer, then $a \cdot 1 = a$.
Inverse	If a is any integer, then $a + (-a) = 0$.	If a is any integer $(a \neq 0)$, then $a \cdot \frac{1}{a} = 1$.
Distributive over Addition	If a, b, and c are integers, then $a(b + c) = ab + ac$.	

1.8 Dividing Integers

There are two cases to consider:

1. When the dividend and the divisor have the same sign
- find the quotient of their absolute values.
- the sign of the quotient is positive.

EXAMPLES:

$(+8) \div (+2) = +4$ $\qquad \frac{+1}{+2} = +\frac{1}{2}$

$(-8) \div (-2) = +4$ $\qquad \frac{-1}{-2} = +\frac{1}{2}$

2. When the dividend and the divisor have different signs
- find the quotient of their absolute values.
- the sign of the quotient is negative.

EXAMPLES:

$(+8) \div (-2) = -4$ $\qquad \frac{-1}{+2} = -\frac{1}{2}$

$(-8) \div (+2) = -4$ $\qquad \frac{+1}{-2} = -\frac{1}{2}$

ALGEBRAIC EXPRESSIONS

Algebraic expressions are meaningful combinations of algebraic symbols and mathematical operations that represent numbers.

2.1 Factors, Exponents, and Roots

- **Factors**
  In $2 \times 5 = 10$, 2 and 5 are called *factors* of 10. This means that 10 is divisible by 2 and 5.

- **Exponents**
  In the expression 3^2, 2 is called the *exponent* or *power* and 3 is called the *base*.

  When the same number is used as a factor twice to form a product as in $3 \times 3 = 9$, it is written as $3^2 = 9$. The result, 9, is called a *perfect square*. In a similar way $2 \times 2 \times 2 = 8$ may be written as $2^3 = 8$. In this case, 2 is used as a factor three times to give a product of 8.

  EXAMPLES: $3x^4 = 3 \cdot x \cdot x \cdot x \cdot x$ where x is the base, 4 is the exponent, and the *numerical coefficient* is 3.
  $(3x)^4 = 3x \cdot 3x \cdot 3x \cdot 3x = 81x^4$ where $3x$ is the base and the exponent is 4.

- **Roots**
  The *square* of a number is the number multiplied by itself or a number raised to the second power.

$$5 \times 5 = 5^2 = 25$$
$$-5 \times -5 = (-5)^2 = 25$$

The *square root* of a number is a number that, when raised to the second power, produces the given number. For example, the square roots of 25 are 5 and -5 because $5^2 = 25$ and $(-5)^2 = 25$.

The principal square root of a positive number is its positive square root. The radical sign, $\sqrt{}$, is used to indicate the principal square root. Therefore $\sqrt{25} = +5$.

Use $-\sqrt{25}$ to indicate the negative square root -5.

The *cube* of a number is the number raised to the third power. $4^3 = 4 \times 4 \times 4 = 64$

The *cube root* of 64, written as $\sqrt[3]{64}$, is 4 since $4^3 = 64$. This same discussion applies to larger powers and roots.

EXAMPLE: What is $\sqrt[3]{8} + \sqrt[5]{32} - \sqrt[3]{27}$?

$$\sqrt[3]{8} = 2, \text{ since } 2^3 = 8$$
$$\sqrt[5]{32} = 2, \text{ since } 2^5 = 32$$
$$\sqrt[3]{27} = 3, \text{ since } 3^3 = 27$$

Thus, $2 + 2 - 3 = 1$.

2.2 Examples of Algebraic Expressions

Arithmetical rules, geometrical facts, or everyday formulas can all be expressed using algebra. In *algebraic expressions*, letters or symbols are used to represent numbers. Some algebraic expressions contain both letters and numbers.

To indicate that the percent of a number can be found by multiplying the rate of percent times the base, we write $P = R \times B$ or $P = RB$. The P stands for part or percent of base, the R stands for rate, and the B stands for base.

Algebraic expressions may include any of the following:

- a. *Numerals:* 4, 0.04, $\frac{1}{4}$, 10^4
- b. *Variables:* a, b, x, y
- c. *Sums:* $x + 2$, $a + z$
- d. *Differences:* $x - 2$, $z - a$
- e. *Products:* $8a$, xy, xy^2, $5(a + b)$
- f. *Quotients:* $\frac{4a}{b}$, $\frac{x}{y^2}$, $\frac{a-2}{-3}$

Since algebraic expressions represent numbers, they may be added, subtracted, multiplied, and divided.

2.3 Writing Algebraic Expressions

In word problems, words and phrases may be written as algebraic expressions. Use a letter to stand for a number.

EXAMPLE: Represent the sum of 8 and a number.
If n represents the number, the expression is $8 + n$.

EXAMPLE: Represent 3 less than 7 times a number.
If a represents the number, then 7 times the number is $7a$, and 3 less than $7a$ is $7a - 3$.

EXAMPLE: Represent 6 divided by a number.
If z represents the number, then 6 divided by z is $\frac{6}{z}$.

EXAMPLE: Represent the product of 5 and a number.
If n represents the number, then the product of 5 and n is $5n$.

2.4 Order of Operations

In a numerical expression, numbers may be joined together by any of the four fundamental operations: addition, subtraction, multiplication, or division. To find the value of an expression without parentheses, do all
1. multiplications and divisions first, from left to right.
2. additions and subtractions next, from left to right.

EXAMPLE: Find the value of $8 - 3 \cdot 2 + 6 \div 2 - 4$.

$$8 - 6 + 3 - 4$$
$$2 + 3 - 4$$
$$5 - 4 = 1$$

If the numerical expression has parentheses, brackets, braces, roots, or powers, do the operations within the parentheses first, starting with the innermost set, and then find the powers and roots.

EXAMPLE:
$$\sqrt{\{[25 - (8 + 2)] \div 5\}^2 + 2 \cdot 8}$$
$$= \sqrt{\{[25 - 10] \div 5\}^2 + 2 \cdot 8}$$
$$= \sqrt{\{15 \div 5\}^2 + 2 \cdot 8}$$
$$= \sqrt{3^2 + 2 \cdot 8}$$
$$= \sqrt{9 + 16}$$
$$= \sqrt{25}$$
$$= 5$$

2.5 Polynomials

Algebraic expressions such as $5x$, $3x - 4$, and $2y^2 + 3y - 1$ are called *polynomials*. Each polynomial is made up of *terms*. A term may be a number, a variable, or the product of a number and one or more variables.

EXAMPLE: The terms in the polynomial $3y^2 - 5y + 4$ are $3y^2$, $-5y$, and 4.

A term in which no variable appears is called a *constant term*. The 4 in the polynomial above is a constant term.

- **Monomial**
  A polynomial of one term is called a *monomial*.

  EXAMPLES: 3, $3a$, b^2 are monomials.

- **Binomial**
  A polynomial of two terms is called a *binomial*.

  EXAMPLES: $3x - y$, $a^2 + b^2$, $y - 5$ are binomials.

- **Trinomial**
  A polynomial of three terms is called a *trinomial*.

  EXAMPLES: $x^2 - 3x + 2$, $x - y + z$ are trinomials.

2.6 Evaluating Algebraic Expressions

The process of finding the numerical value of an algebraic expression for particular values of the variable is called *evaluation*.

EXAMPLE: Find the value of m^3n^2 when $m = -1$ and $n = 2$.
$$m^3n^2 = (-1)^3(2)^2$$
$$= (-1)(4)$$
$$= -4$$

Simplify the algebraic expression first, if you can, before evaluating.

EXAMPLE:

Evaluate $(y^4 + 3y^3 + 4y^2) \div y^2$ when $y = -2$.

To simplify, form a fraction.
$$\frac{y^4 + 3y^3 + 4y^2}{y^2}$$

Then use the distributive property.
$$\frac{y^4}{y^2} + \frac{3y^3}{y^2} + \frac{4y^2}{y^2} = y^2 + 3y + 4$$

Then evaluate. $y^2 + 3y + 4 = (-2)^2 + 3(-2) + 4$
$$= 4 - 6 + 4$$
$$= 2$$

2.7 Adding Polynomials

- **Adding Monomials**
  Monomials can be added if they have *like terms*. Like terms have the same variables with the same exponents for corresponding variables.

  EXAMPLES: $-8xy^2$ and $7xy^2$ are like terms.
  $\qquad\qquad$ $3r$ and $4r^3$ are *not* like terms.

  To add monomials
  - find the sum of the coefficients.
  - multiply by the common variable factors.

  EXAMPLE: Add $-2ab^2 + 6ab^2$.
  $\qquad\qquad (-2) + (+6) = +4$

  Thus, $-2ab^2 + 6ab^2 = +4ab^2$.

- **Adding Polynomials**
  Add the like terms.

  EXAMPLE: Add $5x^2 + 3x - 2$ and $2x^2 - 6x - 4$.
  $$(5x^2 + 3x - 2) + (2x^2 - 6x - 4) =$$
  $$(5x^2 + 2x^2) + (3x - 6x) + (-2 - 4) =$$
  $$7x^2 \quad + \quad (-3x) \quad + \quad (-6) \quad = 7x^2 - 3x - 6$$

2.8 Simplifying Algebraic Expressions

Simplifying algebraic expressions is the process of adding and subtracting like terms. This is also called *combining like terms*.

EXAMPLE: Combine $3x + 5y^2 - x - y^2$.
Since $3x - x = 2x$ and $5y^2 - y^2 = 4y^2$, the expression becomes $2x + 4y^2$. This expression, $2x + 4y^2$, cannot be simplified further.

EXAMPLE: Subtract $\frac{2}{x}$ from $\frac{3}{y}$.
Use the same procedure as for subtracting fractions. The least common denominator (LCD) is the product of x and y or xy.

$$\frac{3}{y} = \frac{3x}{xy} \qquad \frac{2}{x} = \frac{2y}{xy}$$
$$\frac{3}{y} - \frac{2}{x} = \frac{3x}{xy} - \frac{2y}{xy}$$
$$= \frac{3x - 2y}{xy}$$

If an algebraic expression has parentheses, then follow these steps.
1. If the sign before the parentheses is $+$, just remove the parentheses.

EXAMPLE: Simplify $z - 7 + (2z + 3)$.
$$z - 7 + 2z + 3 = 3z - 4$$

2. If the sign before the parentheses is $-$, change the sign of *every* expression inside the parentheses and then remove the parentheses.

EXAMPLE: Simplify $a - 7 - (2a + 3)$.
First change the signs: $2a$ becomes $-2a$ and $+3$ becomes -3.
$$a - 7 - (2a + 3) = a - 7 - 2a - 3$$
$$= -a - 10$$

2.9 Multiplying Algebraic Expressions

- **Law of Exponents for Multiplication**
  For nonnegative integers a and b,
  $$x^a \cdot x^b = x^{a+b}$$

  EXAMPLE: Multiply n^5 by n^2.

  $$n^5 \cdot n^2 = \underbrace{(\underbrace{n \cdot n \cdot n \cdot n \cdot n}_{\text{5 factors}}) \cdot (\underbrace{n \cdot n}_{\text{2 factors}})}_{\text{7 factors}}$$

  $$n^5 \cdot n^2 = n^7$$

- **Monomials**
  To multiply monomials
  - multiply the letters and numbers separately.
  - multiply the result.

  EXAMPLE: Multiply $a^3b^2 \cdot ab^4$.
  $$a^3b^2 \cdot ab^4 = a^3 \cdot a \cdot b^2 \cdot b^4$$
  $$= a^{3+1} \cdot b^{2+4}$$
  $$= a^4b^6$$

  EXAMPLE: Multiply $3a^2 \cdot 2a^3$.
  First, $3 \cdot 2 = 6$, and then $a^2 \cdot a^3 = a^5$.

  Thus, $3a^2 \cdot 2a^3 = 6a^5$.

- **Polynomials**
  To multiply polynomials, use the distributive property.

  EXAMPLE: $x(x + 2) = x \cdot x + x \cdot 2$
  $$= x^2 + 2x$$

  EXAMPLE: $(x - 3)(x + 3) = (x - 3)x + (x - 3)3$
  $$= x^2 - 3x + 3x - 9$$
  $$= x^2 - 9$$

  EXAMPLE: $(x - 4)(x - 5) = (x - 4)x + (x - 4)(-5)$
  $$= x^2 - 4x - 5x + 20$$
  $$= x^2 - 9x + 20$$

EXAMPLE: $(2x - 1)(x + 3) = (2x - 1)x + (2x - 1)3$
$$= 2x^2 - x + 6x - 3$$
$$= 2x^2 + 5x - 3$$

2.10   Dividing Algebraic Expressions

- **Law of Exponents for Division**
  For nonnegative integers a and b, $a \geq b$ and $x \neq 0$,

  $$\frac{x^a}{x^b} = x^{a-b}.$$

  EXAMPLE: Divide x^7 by x^3.

  $$\frac{x^7}{x^3} = x^{7-3} = x^4$$

  EXAMPLE: Divide y^4 by y^4.

  $$\frac{y^4}{y^4} = y^{4-4} = y^0 = 1 \leftarrow$$

  > Any nonzero number raised to the zero power is equal to 1.

  EXAMPLE: Divide $x^2y^3z^5$ by x^2yz^2.

  $$\frac{x^2y^3z^5}{x^2y\,z^2} = x^{2-2} \cdot y^{3-1} \cdot z^{5-2}$$
  $$= x^0 \cdot y^2 \cdot z^3$$
  $$= 1 \cdot y^2 \cdot z^3 = y^2z^3$$

- **Monomial by a Monomial**
  To divide monomials, divide the letters and numbers separately.

  EXAMPLE: Divide $-14a^2b^5$ by $-2ab^3$.
  Form the fraction $\frac{-14a^2b^5}{-2ab^3}$. Divide the numerator and the denominator by the common factors, -2, a, and b^3.

  Thus, $\frac{-14a^2b^5}{-2ab^3} = \frac{-14}{-2} \cdot \frac{a^2}{a} \cdot \frac{b^5}{b^3} = 7ab^2$.

- **Polynomial by a Monomial**
  Use the distributive property to divide a polynomial by a monomial.

  EXAMPLE: Divide $28xy^2 - 14x^2y^5$ by $7xy^2$.
  Form a fraction. $\frac{28xy^2 - 14x^2y^5}{7xy^2}$

  Then use the distributive property. $\frac{28xy^2}{7xy^2} - \frac{14x^2y^5}{7xy^2}$

  Now $\frac{28xy^2}{7xy^2} = 4$, and $\frac{14x^2y^5}{7xy^2} = 2xy^3$.

  Therefore, $\frac{28xy^2 - 14x^2y^5}{7xy^2} = 4 - 2xy^3$.

- **Polynomial by a Binomial**
  • Write both the divisor and the dividend in ascending or descending powers of the variable.
  • Divide the first term of the dividend by the first term of the divisor.

- Multiply this quotient by the divisor.
- Subtract this product from the dividend and bring down the next term.
- Repeat the steps.

EXAMPLE: Divide $n^2 + 7n + 12$ by $n + 4$.

Step 1

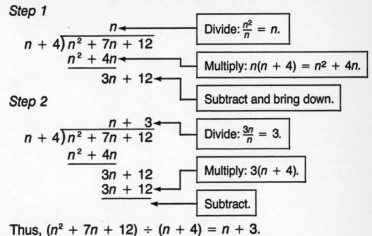

Step 2

$$\begin{array}{r} n + 3 \\ n+4\overline{)n^2 + 7n + 12} \\ n^2 + 4n \\ \hline 3n + 12 \\ 3n + 12 \\ \hline \end{array}$$

Divide: $\frac{3n}{n} = 3$.

Multiply: $3(n + 4)$.

Subtract.

Thus, $(n^2 + 7n + 12) \div (n + 4) = n + 3$.

EXAMPLE: Divide $2n^2 + 3n - 7$ by $n - 1$.

$$\begin{array}{r} 2n + 5 \\ n-1\overline{)2n^2 + 3n - 7} \\ 2n^2 - 2n \\ \hline 5n - 7 \\ 5n - 5 \\ \hline -2 \end{array}$$

Write the remainder over the divisor.

Thus, $(2n^2 + 3n - 7) \div (n - 1) = 2n + 5 - \frac{2}{n - 1}$.

EXAMPLE: Divide $9b^2 - 30b + 24$ by $3b - 4$.

$$\begin{array}{r} 3b - 6 \\ 3b-4\overline{)9b^2 - 30b + 24} \\ 9b^2 - 12b \\ \hline -18b + 24 \\ -18b + 24 \\ \hline \end{array}$$

Thus, $(9b^2 - 30b + 24) \div (3b - 4) = 3b - 6$.

2.11 New Operations

Some problems in evaluation are presented differently. Up to this point, we operated on two numbers to get a third number: $3 + 2 = 5$ or $3 \times 2 = 6$. Many other operations could be defined. These operations can be defined by algebraic expressions. Remember: Division by 0 is undefined, so the denominator of a fraction cannot be 0.

EXAMPLE: If for all numbers x and y, $x \neq 0$, $y \neq 0$, and $x \bigcirc y = \frac{x + y}{xy}$, then evaluate $5 \bigcirc 3$.

To find $5 \bigcirc 3$, evaluate $\frac{x + y}{xy}$ with $x = 5$ and $y = 3$.

Thus, $5 \bigcirc 3 = \frac{5 + 3}{(5)(3)} = \frac{8}{15}$.

EXAMPLE: If for all numbers x and y, $x \neq 0$, $y \neq 0$, and $x * y = \frac{y}{x} - \frac{x}{y}$, then evaluate $2 * 5$.

To find $2 * 5$, evaluate $\frac{y}{x} - \frac{x}{y}$ with $x = 2$ and $y = 5$.

Thus, $2 * 5 = \frac{5}{2} - \frac{2}{5}$
$$= \frac{25}{10} - \frac{4}{10} = \frac{21}{10} \text{ or } 2\frac{1}{10}$$

FACTORING

The factors of an expression are two or more expressions whose product is the original expression. *To factor* an expression is to write the expression as the product of its factors.

3.1 Prime and Composite Numbers

A *prime* number is any integer greater than 1 that is divisible only by itself and 1; that is, it has only two different factors. The integer 2 is the only *even* prime number.

EXAMPLE: The first 8 prime numbers are 2, 3, 5, 7, 11, 13, 17, and 19.

A *composite* number is any number that has more than two factors. The number 1 is neither prime nor composite since it has only one factor.

EXAMPLE: 12 is a composite number since 2 is a factor of 12, 3 is a factor of 12, and 1, 4, 6, and 12 are factors of 12.

3.2 Prime Factorization

If a factor of a number is a prime number, it is called a *prime factor*. The *prime factorization* of a number is the product of all the prime factors of the number. The prime factors may be found using a factor tree.

EXAMPLE: Find the prime factorization of 36.

Use a factor tree: 36

$$3 \times 12$$

$$3 \times 3 \times 4$$

$$3 \times 3 \times 2 \times 2$$

Thus, the prime factorization of 36 is $3 \times 3 \times 2 \times 2$, or $2^2 \cdot 3^2$.

3.3 Greatest Common Factor (GCF)

A factor that divides each term of an expression is called a common factor. To factor an algebraic expression, find the *greatest common factor* of all the terms in the expression. Then divide each term by the GCF. The quotient is the other factor. Write the expression as the product of the two factors.

EXAMPLE: Factor $3x + 6$.
3 is the GCF of both $3x$ and 6, so divide $3x + 6$ by 3.

$$\frac{3x + 6}{3} = \frac{3x}{3} + \frac{6}{3}$$
$$= x + 2$$

Therefore, $3x + 6 = 3(x + 2)$.

EXAMPLE: Factor $4x^2 - 8x$.
$4x$ is the GCF of both $4x^2$ and $8x$, so divide $4x^2 - 8x$ by $4x$.

$$\frac{4x^2 - 8x}{4x} = \frac{4x^2}{4x} - \frac{8x}{4x}$$
$$= x - 2$$

Therefore, $4x^2 - 8x = 4x(x - 2)$.

3.4 Difference of Two Squares

If an algebraic expression has two terms consisting of one perfect square minus another perfect square, the expression is the *difference of two perfect squares*.

$9a^2 - 16$ is an example of the difference of two perfect squares. $9a^2$ is a perfect square since $(3a)(3a) = 9a^2$. 16 is a perfect square since $(4)(4) = 16$.

To factor the difference of two squares, form the sum and the difference of the square root of each number. Write the answer as the product of these two factors.

EXAMPLE: Factor $9a^2 - 16$.
Find the principal square root of each perfect square.

$$\sqrt{9a^2} = 3a \qquad\qquad \sqrt{16} = 4$$

Form the sum and the difference of the square roots, $3a + 4$ and $3a - 4$.

Thus, $9a^2 - 16 = (3a + 4)(3a - 4)$.

Sometimes a trinomial can be factored into two binomials.

EXAMPLE: $x^2 - 3x - 4 = (x - 4)(x + 1)$
$x^2 - 3x - 4$ is an example of a trinomial; $x - 4$ and $x + 1$, the factors of $x^2 - 3x - 4$, are binomials.

Not all trinomials can be factored into binomials. It is not easy to determine which trinomials can be factored without attempting to factor the expression. The method which is widely used requires trial and error.

● **Factoring $x^2 + bx + c$ where b and c are numbers.**
Find the factors of the first term. $(x\ \ )(x\ \ )$
Find the factors of c whose sum is b. (This requires trial and error.) Then write the trinomial as the product of the two factors.

EXAMPLE: Factor $z^2 + 6z + 8$.
Write the factors of the first term. $(z\ \ )(z\ \ )$
Find all the factors of $+8$.

$$+1, +8 \qquad +2, +4$$
$$-1, -8 \qquad -2, -4$$

Choose the pair of factors whose sum is the middle term, $+6$. The only pair of factors that gives a sum of 6 is $+2$ and $+4$.

Thus, $z^2 + 6z + 8 = (z + 2)(z + 4)$.

EXAMPLE: Factor $t^2 - 5t + 4$.
Write the factors of the first term. $(t\ \ )(t\ \ )$
Find all the factors of $+4$.

$$+1, +4 \qquad +2, +2$$
$$-1, -4 \qquad -2, -2$$

Choose the pair of factors whose sum is the middle term, -5. The only pair of factors that gives a sum of -5 is -1 and -4.

Thus, $t^2 - 5t + 4 = (t - 1)(t - 4)$.

EXAMPLE: Factor $y^2 - 5y - 14$.
Write the factors of the first term. $(y\ \ )(y\ \ )$
Find all the factors of -14.

$$-1, +14 \qquad -2, +7$$
$$+1, -14 \qquad +2, -7$$

Choose the pair of factors whose sum is the middle term, -5. The only pair of factors that gives the sum of -5 is -7 and $+2$

Thus, $y^2 - 5y - 14 = (y - 7)(y + 2)$.

- **Factoring $ax^2 + bx + c$ where a, b, and c are numbers, and $a > 1$.**

Find all possible factors of ax^2 and of c. Then form possible pairs of binomial factors. Multiply these pairs to find the pair whose product is the trinomial.

EXAMPLE: Factor $2x^2 + x - 6$.
The factors of $2x^2$ are x and $2x$.
$$2x^2 + x - 6 = (x \quad)(2x \quad)$$

The factors of -6 are

$-1, +6 \qquad +2, -3$
$+1, -6 \qquad -2, +3$

All possible pairs of factors are

1. $(x - 1)(2x + 6)$ 2. $(x + 6)(2x - 1)$
3. $(x + 1)(2x - 6)$ 4. $(x - 6)(2x + 1)$
5. $(x + 2)(2x - 3)$ 6. $(x - 3)(2x + 2)$
7. $(x - 2)(2x + 3)$ 8. $(x + 3)(2x - 2)$

Note: If the trinomial does not have a common factor, then each factor cannot have a common factor. This simplifies your work since choices 1, 3, 6, and 8 above are eliminated from the possible pairs of factors.

1. $2x + 6 = 2(x + 3)$ 6. $2x + 2 = 2(x + 1)$
3. $2x - 6 = 2(x - 3)$ 8. $2x - 2 = 2(x - 1)$

Multiply the remaining pairs of binomials to find the pair whose product is $2x^2 + x - 6$. The correct pair is $(x + 2)(2x - 3)$ since

$$
\begin{aligned}
(x + 2)(2x - 3) &= (x + 2)2x + (x + 2)(-3) \\
&= 2x^2 + 4x - 3x - 6 \\
&= 2x^2 + x - 6
\end{aligned}
$$

3.6 Complete Factoring

To factor an expression completely is to factor it into expressions that cannot be factored any further.

EXAMPLE: Factor completely $2x^2 - 32$.
Look for a common factor and divide.

$$2x^2 - 32 = 2(x^2 - 16)$$

$x^2 - 16$ is the difference of two squares and can still be factored into $(x + 4)(x - 4)$.

Thus, $2x^2 - 32 = 2(x + 4)(x - 4)$.

EXAMPLE: Factor completely $a^4 - b^4$
$a^4 - b^4$ is the difference of two squares, so
$$a^4 - b^4 = (a^2 - b^2)(a^2 + b^2)$$

$a^2 - b^2$ is the difference of two squares, so
$$a^2 - b^2 = (a + b)(a - b)$$

Thus, $a^4 - b^4 = (a^2 + b^2)(a + b)(a - b)$

EQUATIONS

An *equation* is a mathematical sentence that states that two expressions are equal.

EXAMPLES: $5 + 6 = 11$, $3x + 1 = 10$, and formulas such as $P = R \times B$ (Percent = Rate $\times$ Base).

In the equation $3x + 1 = 10$, the *members* of the equation are $3x + 1$ and 10. The equals sign indicates that the two members of the equation have the same value, 10.

To solve the equation $3x + 1 = 10$, look for the value of the variable x that makes $3x + 1 = 10$ a true statement. Since the value $x = 3$ will make this a true statement, 3 is the *solution* or 3 is said to *satisfy* the equation.

4.1 Equivalence Relations

- **Reflexive**
  Any number is equal to itself.

  EXAMPLE: For any number a, $a = a$.

- **Symmetric**
  An equality can be read from right to left as well as from left to right.

  EXAMPLE: For any numbers a and b, if $a = b$, then $b = a$.

- **Transitive**
  Two numbers are equal to each other if each number is equal to a third number.

  EXAMPLE: For any numbers a, b, and c, if $a = b$ and $b = c$, then $a = c$.

4.2 Properties of Equality

- **Substitution**
  A number or an expression may be substituted for its equal in any equation.

  EXAMPLE: Find the sum $20 + 9 + 6$.
  First, group the addends:
  $$(20 + 9) + 6$$

  Since $20 + 9 = 29$, we may substitute 29 for $20 + 9$

  Thus, $(20 + 9) + 6 = 29 + 6$.

  By substituting 35 for $29 + 6$, we find that
  $$20 + 9 + 6 = 35$$

EXAMPLE: If $x = 3y$ and $5y + x = 7$, then $3y$ can be substituted for x in the equation $5y + x = 7$.

Therefore, $5y + x = 7$.
$$5y + (3y) = 7 \text{ or } 5y + 3y = 7$$

- **Addition**
  If the same quantity is added to both members of the equation, the resulting expressions are equal.

  Therefore, for integers a, b, and c, if $a = b$, then $a + c = b + c$.

  EXAMPLE: $y - 3 = 9$
  Add 3 to both sides of the equation.
  $$y - 3 + 3 = 9 + 3$$
  $$y = 12$$

- **Subtraction**
  If the same quantity is subtracted from both members of the equation, the resulting expressions are equal.

  Therefore, for integers a, b, and c, if $a = b$, then $a - c = b - c$.

  EXAMPLE: $a + 4 = 12$
  Subtract 4 from both sides of the equation.
  $$a + 4 - 4 = 12 - 4$$
  $$a = 8$$

- **Multiplication**
  If both members of the equation are multiplied by the same quantity, the resulting expressions are equal.

  Therefore, for integers a, b, and c, if $a = b$, then $ac = bc$.

  EXAMPLE: $\frac{x}{5} = \frac{3}{10}$
  Multiply both sides of the equation by 5.
  $$(5)\frac{x}{5} = \frac{3}{10}(5)$$
  $$x = \frac{3}{\overset{}{\underset{2}{10}}} \times \overset{1}{5} = \frac{3}{2} \text{ or } 1\frac{1}{2}$$

- **Division**
  If both members of the equation are divided by the same nonzero quantity, the resulting expressions are equal.

  Therefore, for integers a, b, and c ($c \neq 0$), if $a = b$, then $\frac{a}{c} = \frac{b}{c}$.

  EXAMPLE: $16m = 8$
  Divide both sides of the equation by 16.
  $$\frac{16m}{16} = \frac{8}{16}$$
  $$m = \frac{1}{2}$$

4.3 Using Properties of Equality to Solve Equations

The four properties of equality are used to get the variable alone on one side of the equation and all numbers or constant terms on the other side.

● **More Than One Operation**
Sometimes more than one property of equality must be used to solve an equation. When that occurs, addition or subtraction is used before multiplication or division.

EXAMPLE: Solve $3x + 5 = 26$.
First, subtract 5 from both sides of the equation.
$$3x + 5 = 26$$
$$3x + 5 - 5 = 26 - 5$$
$$3x = 21$$
Then, divide both sides of the equation by 3.
$$\frac{3x}{3} = \frac{21}{3}$$
$$x = 7$$

● **Checking the Solution**
After solving an equation, the solution should be checked to make sure it is correct. Substitute the value found for the variable in the equation and then evaluate the expressions in each member of the equation to see if they are equal.

To check the solution in the above example, substitute 7 for x in the given equation.
$$3x + 5 = 26$$
$$3(7) + 5 \stackrel{?}{=} 26$$
$$21 + 5 \stackrel{?}{=} 26$$
$$26 = 26$$

Thus, the solution $x = 7$ is correct.

● **Combining Like Terms**
When there are like terms in the same member of the equation, they should be combined first before solving the equation.

EXAMPLE: Solve $13y - 3y = 20$.
Combine $13y$ and $-3y$.
$$10y = 20$$
Divide both sides of the equation by 10.
$$y = 2$$
To check the solution, substitute 2 for y in the given equation.
$$13y - 3y = 20$$
$$13(2) - 3(2) \stackrel{?}{=} 20$$
$$26 - 6 \stackrel{?}{=} 20$$
$$20 = 20$$

Thus, the solution $y = 2$ is correct.

EXAMPLE: Solve $4a + 3 - 2a = 8$.
Combine $4a$ and $-2a$.
$$2a + 3 = 8$$
Subtract 3 from both sides of the equation.
$$2a + 3 - 3 = 8 - 3$$
$$2a = 5$$
Divide both sides of the equation by 2.
$$\frac{2a}{2} = \frac{5}{2}$$
$$a = \frac{5}{2} \text{ or } 2\frac{1}{2}$$
Check by substituting $\frac{5}{2}$ for a in the equation.
$$4a + 3 - 2a = 8$$
$$4\left(\frac{5}{2}\right) + 3 - 2\left(\frac{5}{2}\right) \stackrel{?}{=} 8$$
$$10 + 3 - 5 \stackrel{?}{=} 8$$
$$8 = 8$$

Thus, the solution $a = \frac{5}{2}$ or $2\frac{1}{2}$ is correct.

EXAMPLE: Solve $5a - 3 = 11 - 2a$
Add $2a$ to both sides of the equation.
$$5a - 3 + 2a = 11 - 2a + 2a$$
Combine like terms.
$$7a - 3 = 11$$
Add 3 to both sides of the equation.
$$7a - 3 + 3 = 11 + 3$$
$$7a = 14$$
Divide both sides of the equation by 7.
$$\frac{7a}{7} = \frac{14}{7}$$
$$a = 2$$
Check by substituting 2 for a in the equation.
$$5a - 3 = 11 - 2a$$
$$5(2) - 3 \stackrel{?}{=} 11 - 2(2)$$
$$10 - 3 \stackrel{?}{=} 11 - 4$$
$$7 = 7$$

Thus, the solution $a = 2$ is correct.

4.4 Quadratic Equations

A quadratic equation is an equation in which the highest power of the variable is 2.

EXAMPLES: $y^2 - 3y + 1 = 0$, $3y^2 = 5$, and $x^2 = 5x - 2$.

Some quadratic equations can be solved using the method for factoring a polynomial.

EXAMPLE: Solve the equation $a^2 - 36 = 0$.
Factor the expression $a^2 - 36$ using the difference of two squares.
$$(a - 6)(a + 6) = 0$$

Since the product of the two factors is zero, then one of the factors is zero or both factors are zero.

So, $a - 6 = 0$ or $a + 6 = 0$

$a - 6 + 6 = 0 + 6$ $a + 6 - 6 = 0 - 6$

$a = 6$ $a = -6$

The solution is either $a = 6$ or $a = -6$.

Check by substituting both 6 and -6 for a in the equation.

For $a = 6$: $a^2 - 36 = 0$ For $a = -6$: $a^2 - 36 = 0$

$(6)^2 - 36 \overset{?}{=} 0$ $(-6)^2 - 36 \overset{?}{=} 0$

$36 - 36 \overset{?}{=} 0$ $36 - 36 \overset{?}{=} 0$

$0 = 0$ $0 = 0$

Thus, $a = 6$ and $a = -6$ are both solutions.

EXAMPLE: Solve the equation $x^2 = 5x$.

Bring all the members onto one side of the equation by subtracting 5x from both sides of the equation.

$$x^2 - 5x = 5x - 5x$$
$$x^2 - 5x = 0$$

Factor the expression $x^2 - 5x$ using the GCF.

$$x(x - 5) = 0$$

Set each of the factors equal to zero.

$$x = 0 \text{ or } x - 5 = 0$$
$$x = 5$$

The solution is $x = 0$ or $x = 5$.

Check by substituting both 0 and 5 for x in the equation.

For $x = 0$: $x^2 = 5x$ For $x = 5$: $x^2 = 5x$

$(0)^2 \overset{?}{=} 5(0)$ $5^2 \overset{?}{=} 5(5)$

$0 = 0$ $25 = 25$

Thus, $x = 0$ and $x = 5$ are both solutions.

EXAMPLE: Solve the equation $x^2 = 3x + 4$.

Bring all the members onto one side of the equation by subtracting $3x + 4$ from both sides of the equation.

$$x^2 - 3x - 4 = 3x + 4 - 3x - 4$$
$$x^2 - 3x - 4 = 0$$

Factor the trinomial $x^2 - 3x - 4$.

$$(x - 4)(x + 1) = 0$$

Set each of the factors equal to 0.

$$x - 4 = 0 \quad \text{or} \quad x + 1 = 0$$
$$x = 4 \qquad\qquad x = -1$$

The solution is $x = 4$ or $x = -1$.

Check by substituting 4 and -1 for x in the equation.

For $x = 4$: $x^2 = 3x + 4$ For $x = -1$: $x^2 = 3x + 4$

$4^2 \overset{?}{=} 3(4) + 4$ $(-1)^2 \overset{?}{=} 3(-1) + 4$

$16 \overset{?}{=} 12 + 4$ $1 \overset{?}{=} -3 + 4$

$16 = 16$ $1 = 1$

Thus, $x = 4$ and $x = -1$ are both solutions.

If an equation has more than one variable, there may be more than one solution for the variables. The value of one variable will depend on the value of the other variables.

EXAMPLE: Solve the equation $x + 2y = 8$.
The solution of the equation, $x + 2y = 8$, is a *number pair*. One number pair which satisfies this equation is $x = 2$ and $y = 3$, since

$$x + 2y = 8$$
$$(2) + 2(3) \stackrel{?}{=} 8$$
$$2 + 6 \stackrel{?}{=} 8$$
$$8 = 8$$

The number pair is conveniently written as (x,y) or $(2,3)$. This pair of numbers is called an *ordered pair* since the order of the numbers is important.

There are an infinite number of ordered pairs which satisfy this equation. Some of these are $(4,2)$, $(0,4)$, $(-2,5)$, $(12,-2)$, and so on. This set of possible solutions is called the *solution set* of the equation.

By choosing any number for x, you can find the number pair which satisfies the equation. For example, if $x = 3$,
$$x + 2y = 8$$
$$3 + 2y = 8$$
Subtract 3 from both sides of the equation.
$$3 + 2y - 3 = 8 - 3$$
$$2y = 5$$
Divide both sides of the equation by 2.
$$\frac{2y}{2} = \frac{5}{2}$$
$$y = 2\frac{1}{2}$$
Another solution is $(3, 2\frac{1}{2})$.

If the value of x is not given you could not solve for y.
In problems like this, you might be asked to solve for one variable in terms of the other.

EXAMPLE: Solve $2x + 3 = 5y$ for x in terms of y.
Subtract 3 from both sides of the equation.
$$2x + 3 - 3 = 5y - 3$$
$$2x = 5y - 3$$
Divide both sides of the equation by 2.
$$\frac{2x}{2} = \frac{5y - 3}{2}$$
$$x = \frac{5y - 3}{2}$$

You can solve the same equation for y in terms of x.
$$2x + 3 = 5y$$
Divide both sides of the equation by 5.
$$\frac{2x + 3}{5} = \frac{5y}{5}$$
$$\frac{2x + 3}{5} = y$$

4.6   Solving Two Equations with Two Variables

Sometimes the solution of one equation is used to solve another equation.

EXAMPLE: If $2x + 3 = 5y$ and $x = 6$, find y.
Substitute 6 for x in the equation.
$$2x + 3 = 5y$$
$$2(6) + 3 = 5y$$
$$12 + 3 = 5y$$
$$15 = 5y$$
Divide both sides of the equation by 5.
$$\frac{15}{5} = \frac{5y}{5}$$
$$3 = y$$
Check by substituting 6 for x and 3 for y in $2x + 3 = 5y$.
$$2x + 3 = 5y$$
$$2(6) + 3 \stackrel{?}{=} 5(3)$$
$$12 + 3 \stackrel{?}{=} 15$$
$$15 = 15$$

Thus, $y = 3$ is the correct solution.

EXAMPLE: If $2x + y = 5$ and $y = 3 - x$, find x and y.
Substitute the value $3 - x$ for y from the second equation in the first equation.
$$2x + y = 5$$
$$2x + (3 - x) = 5$$
Remove the parentheses.
$$2x + 3 - x = 5$$
Combine like terms.
$$x + 3 = 5$$
Subtract 3 from both sides of the equation.
$$x + 3 - 3 = 5 - 3$$
$$x = 2$$
Substitute 2 for x in either equation.
$$y = 3 - x$$
$$y = 3 - 2$$
$$y = 1$$
Check by substituting 2 for x and 1 for y in $2x + y = 5$
$$2x + y = 5$$
$$2(2) + 1 \stackrel{?}{=} 5$$
$$4 + 1 \stackrel{?}{=} 5$$
$$5 = 5$$

Thus, $x = 2$ and $y = 1$ is the correct solution

4.7   The Coordinate Plane

Since every point on a plane can be represented as a pair of numbers, or as a set of coordinates, the plane is called a *coordinate plane.* Two number lines are drawn perpendicular to each other. The horizontal line is called the *x-axis* and the vertical line is called the *y-axis.* The two axes (plural of axis) meet at the 0 point on each number line. This point is called the *origin.*

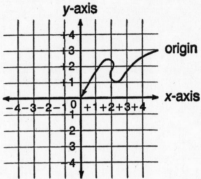

4.8   The Ordered Pair

The pair of numbers that locates a point in the coordinate plane is called an *ordered pair.* The ordered pair names the coordinates of the point.

To name a point using an ordered pair, first draw a perpendicular from the point to the *x*-axis. The number on the *x*-axis is called the *x-coordinate* of the point.

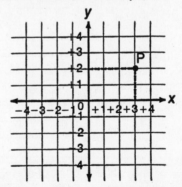

The line segment intersects the *x*-axis at the point +3.

Then draw a perpendicular from the point to the *y*-axis. The number on the *y*-axis is called the *y-coordinate* of the point.

This line segment intersects the *y*-axis at the point +2.

To name a point, the x-coordinate is written first, and then the y-coordinate after it in the form (x,y). The general form for labeling a point using an ordered pair is (x,y).

The ordered pair (3,2) gives the exact location of point P in the preceding figure.

EXAMPLE: Locate points P, Q, R, and S with ordered pairs.

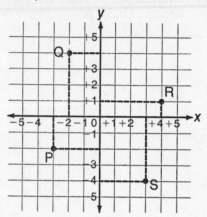

The figure above shows the location of points P (−3, −2); Q (−2, 4); R (4, 1); and S (3, −4).

EXAMPLE: Graph the points whose ordered pairs are (2, 3) and (3, 2).

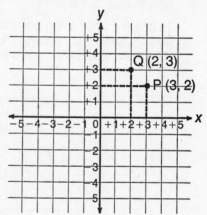

(2, 3) locates point Q and (3, 2) locates point P.

4.9 Points on the Axes

- (0, 0) is the ordered pair for the origin.
- The x-coordinate is 0 for any point on the y-axis.
- The y-coordinate is 0 for any point on the x-axis.

EXAMPLE:

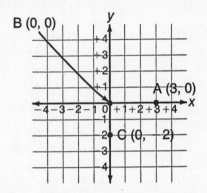

Point B, the origin, has the coordinates (0, 0).
Point C, a point on the y-axis, is (0, −2).
Point A, a point on the x-axis, is (3, 0).

4.10 Graphing a Linear Equation

An equation whose graph is a straight line is called a *linear equation*. A linear equation with two variables can be graphed in the coordinate plane. The graph is the set of all points corresponding to the pairs of numbers belonging to the solution set of the equation.

EXAMPLE: Draw the graph of the equation $2x + y = 4$.

There are many ordered pairs belonging to the solution set of this equation. Choose any value for x and find the corresponding value for y. Three of the solutions are shown in the chart.

x	2x + y = 4	y	(x, y)
−1	$2(-1) + y = 4$	6	(−1, 6)
	$y = 6$		
0	$2(0) + y = 4$	4	(0, 4)
	$y = 4$		
3	$2(3) + y = 4$	−2	(3, −2)
	$y = -2$		

Graph these coordinate pairs on the coordinate plane and connect the points.

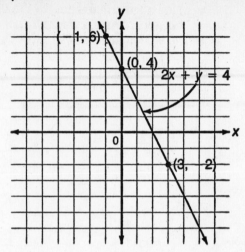

The straight line above is the graph of the solution set of $2x + y = 4$.

4.11 Graphing Two Linear Equations

The solution set of a pair of equations can be graphed on a coordinate plane. Graph each equation separately. Then locate the point of intersection of the two lines. The ordered pair for this point is the solution set for the pair of equations.

EXAMPLE: Find the solution set of $x - y = 3$ and $2x + 3y = 6$.

Find three ordered pairs for each equation.

x	x − y = 3	y	(x, y)
−1	(−1) − y = 3	−4	(−1, −4)
0	0 − y = 3	−3	(0, −3)
4	(4) − y = 3	1	(4, 1)

x	2x + 3y = 6	y	(x, y)
−3	2(−3) + 3y = 6	4	(−3, 4)
0	2(0) + 3y = 6	2	(0, 2)
6	2(6) + 3y = 6	−2	(6, −2)

Graph the coordinate pairs for each line on the coordinate plane.

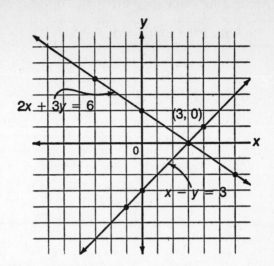

The coordinate pair (3, 0), the point of intersection, is the solution set of $x - y = 3$ and $2x + 3y = 6$.

Check by substituting 3 for x and 0 for y in each equation.

$$x - y = 3 \qquad \text{and} \qquad 2x + 3y = 6$$
$$3 - 0 \overset{?}{=} 3 \qquad\qquad\qquad 2(3) + 3(0) \overset{?}{=} 6$$
$$3 = 3 \qquad\qquad\qquad\qquad 6 + 0 \overset{?}{=} 6$$
$$\qquad\qquad\qquad\qquad\qquad\qquad\quad 6 = 6$$

RATIO AND PROPORTION

A *ratio* is the quotient of two nonzero numbers; $\frac{a}{b}$ is called the ratio of a to b.

5.1 Ratio

A *ratio* may be written as $2:3$,   2 to 3,   or as $\frac{2}{3}$.

In a ratio, the two numbers compared are called the *terms* of the ratio. The ratios $8:12$, $4:6$, and $2:3$ are *equivalent* ratios. The ratio $2:3$ is called the *simplest form* of the ratio $8:12$ because its terms, 2 and 3, have only the common factor 1.

When a ratio is used to compare two like measures, such as two measures of length, the quantities should first be expressed in the same unit of measure.

EXAMPLE: Write the ratio of 2 inches to 2 feet.
The ratio of 2 inches to 2 feet is the ratio of 2 inches to 24 inches, or $2:24$.

Since a ratio may be represented as a fraction, ratios can be operated on in the same manner as fractions.

Therefore, $2:24 = 1:12$ because
$$\frac{2}{24} = \frac{1}{12}$$

5.2 Using Ratios to Compare Quantities

If two quantities are related by a formula, a change in one quantity may cause the second quantity to change. To find the change in one quantity, given the other, form this ratio:

New value : Original value

EXAMPLE: The area of a rectangle is *bh* where *b* is the base and *h* is the height. What happens to the area if the base is tripled and the height is halved?

The original value of the area is *bh*. The new base is triple the original base, or 3*b*. The new height is one half the original height, or $\frac{1}{2}h$. The new area is $(3b)(\frac{1}{2}h)$ or $\frac{3}{2}bh$.

The ratio: $\dfrac{\text{New area}}{\text{Original area}} = \dfrac{\frac{3}{2}bh}{bh} = \dfrac{\frac{3}{2}}{1} = \dfrac{3}{2}$

5.3 The Meaning of Proportion

Since the ratio $\frac{2}{3}$ is equivalent to the ratio $\frac{6}{9}$, you may write the statement $\frac{2}{3} = \frac{6}{9}$. A statement of equality between two ratios is called a *proportion*. This proportion may also be expressed as 2 : 3 = 6 : 9.

A proportion has four terms. In the proportion 2 : 3 = 6 : 9, 2 is the first term, 3 is the second term, 6 is the third term, and 9 is the fourth term.

The first and fourth terms are called the *extremes*; the second and third terms are called the *means*.

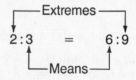

5.4 Finding the Unknown Term of a Proportion

When three of the four terms of a proportion are known, the fourth term may be found by using the rule: In any proportion, the product of the means is equal to the product of the extremes.

EXAMPLE: For what value of *y* will $\frac{y}{12} = \frac{9}{16}$?
The product of the extremes is 16*y*. The product of the means is 9 · 12 or 108.

Then, $16y = 108$

Divide each side of the equation by 16.

$$\frac{16y}{16} = \frac{108}{16}$$

$$y = 6\frac{12}{16} \text{ or } 6\frac{3}{4}$$

EXAMPLE: Find the number if $\frac{3}{8}$ of $\frac{5}{6}$ is equal to $\frac{2}{3}$ of the number.

Write an equation using n to represent the missing number and then solve.

$$\frac{3}{8}\left(\frac{5}{6}\right) = \frac{2}{3}(n)$$

$$\frac{\overset{1}{\cancel{3}}}{8} \cdot \frac{5}{\underset{2}{\cancel{6}}} = \frac{2n}{3}$$

$$\frac{5}{16} = \frac{2n}{3}$$

The product of the extremes is $5 \cdot 3$ or 15. The product of the means is $16 \cdot 2n = 32n$.

$$32n = 15$$

$$n = \frac{15}{32}$$

5.5   Using Proportions to Solve Problems

Proportions can be used to solve rate problems.

EXAMPLE: Two cans of soup cost $.69. At that rate, what is the cost of 12 cans of soup?

Represent the cost of 12 cans of soup by x. Then write the proportion.

$$\frac{2}{69} = \frac{12}{x}$$

$$2x = 828$$

$$x = 414$$

The cost of 12 cans of soup is $4.14.

A proportion can be used to solve scale problems. Be sure that the ratios of the two measurements compare the same units.

EXAMPLE: On a map, 1 cm represents 8 km. Two cities are 4.2 cm apart on the map. What is the actual distance between the cities?

Let d = the actual distance between the two cities. Then write and solve a proportion.

$$\frac{1}{8} = \frac{4.2}{d}$$

$$d = 33.6$$

The actual distance between the cities is 33.6 km.

EXAMPLE: On a scale drawing, if 6 centimeters represent 9 meters, how many centimeters represent 2 meters 7 centimeters? (100 centimeters = 1 meter)
The measurement 2 meters 7 centimeters must first be expressed in meters.
Let y = the number of meters in 7 cm. Write and solve a proportion.

$$\frac{100}{1} = \frac{7}{y}$$
$$100y = 7$$
$$y = \frac{7}{100} = 0.07$$

Therefore, 2 meters 7 centimeters = 2.07 meters.

Now, let x = the number of centimeters needed to represent 2.07 meters on the map. Write and solve a proportion.

$$\frac{6}{9} = \frac{x}{2.07}$$
$$9x = 12.42$$
$$x = 1.38$$

Therefore, 1.38 centimeters are required to represent 2 meters 7 centimeters.

Proportions can also be used to solve problems involving percents.

EXAMPLE: A school baseball team won 19 games of the 25 games it played. What percent of its games did the team win?

Let n = the percent of games the team won.
Recall that $n\%$ may be written as $\frac{n}{100}$.

Then,
$$\frac{19}{25} = \frac{n}{100}$$
$$25n = 1900$$
$$n = 76$$

The team won 76% of its games.

EXAMPLE: There are 2400 students registered in the high school. The absence recorded one day was 8% of the students registered. How many students were present that day?

Let x = the number of students present. If 8% of the students were absent, then 92% of the students were present. Write and solve a proportion.

$$\frac{x}{2400} = \frac{92}{100}$$
$$100x = 220,800$$
$$x = 2208$$

There were 2208 students present.

EXAMPLE: Florence sold 21 tickets to a school football game. This number was 5% of all the tickets sold by students. How many tickets were sold by students?

Let x = the total number of tickets sold by students. Write and solve a proportion.

$$\frac{21}{x} = \frac{5}{100}$$
$$5x = 2100$$
$$x = 420$$

Thus, 420 tickets were sold by students.

PROBABILITY

Probability is an estimate of an event's happening by an analysis of the ways it may happen or fail to happen.

6.1 Fundamental Principle

If an event can occur in r ways and another event in s ways, then the two events can be done in succession in $r \times s$ ways.

EXAMPLE: A man lost 2 shoes on vacation leaving him with 5 right shoes and 3 left shoes. In how many ways can he make up a pair of shoes?

List all the possibilities by writing the right shoes as R_1, R_2, R_3, R_4, and R_5 and the left shoes as L_1, L_2, and L_3. Then write down all the choices using a diagram.

R_1 can pair with any of the three left shoes, as can R_2, and so on. Altogether there are 5×3 or 15 ways.

This principle can be extended to more than two operations or events.

EXAMPLE: In how many ways can a librarian place 9 different books on a shelf?

The first book can be any one of 9, the second any one of 8, the third any one of 7, and so on. Therefore, the number of possible arrangements is

$$9 \times 8 \times 7 \times 6 \times 5 \times 4 \times 3 \times 2 \times 1.$$

Another way of writing this product is 9! which is read as 9 *factorial.*

Thus, $9! = 362,880$

6.2 Probability of a Single Event

If an event can happen in *s* ways and fail to happen in *f* ways, then the probability that it will happen is $\frac{s}{s+f}$. The probability that it will *not* happen is $\frac{f}{s+f}$.

EXAMPLE: If in a toss of a coin a head can happen in 1 way and fail to happen in 1 way, the probability that a head will happen in 1 trial is $\frac{1}{1+1}$ or $\frac{1}{2}$.

The probability of an event ranges from 0 to 1. If the probability of an event occurring is 0, the event certainly will not occur. If the probability of an event occurring is 1, the event is certain.

A *random sampling* means that all members of the group have an equal chance of being chosen.

EXAMPLE: One ball is drawn at random from a box containing 3 red balls, 2 white balls, and 4 blue balls. What is the probability that it is red?

$$P = \frac{\text{ways of drawing 1 out of 3 red balls}}{\text{ways of drawing 1 out of 9 balls}} = \frac{3}{9} = \frac{1}{3}$$

EXAMPLE: What is the chance of obtaining 2 heads in successive throws of a coin?

Make a table.

First Throw		Second Throw	
Head	(H)	Head	(H)
Head	(H)	Tail	(T)
Tail	(T)	Head	(H)
Tail	(T)	Tail	(T)

There are 4 equally likely possibilities and only 1 of them is favorable. Thus, the chance of 2 heads is $\frac{1}{4}$.

INEQUALITIES

A mathematical sentence which indicates that two algebraic expressions do *not* have the same number is called an *inequality*.

7.1 Meaning of Inequalities

Some of the signs of inequality are

$\neq$ is not equal to	$\leq$ is less than or equal to
$<$ is less than	$\geq$ is greater than or equal to
$>$ is greater than	

EXAMPLES $5y > 1$ $x < -2$, $z \neq 0$

The inequalities $x > 0$ and $x < 0$ are often written to indicate whether the set of numbers is positive or negative. If a number x is positive, it is written as $x > 0$, and if x is negative it is written as $x < 0$.

7.2 Properties of Inequalities

- **Order Property**
  For any two integers a and b, one and only one of the following is true:

  $$a = b \qquad a > b \qquad a < b$$

  EXAMPLES: $3 = 3 \qquad 3 > 2 \qquad -5 < -4$

  For any two integers a and b, if $a > b$ then $b < a$.

  EXAMPLES: If $5 > 2$, then $2 < 5$.
  If $-1 > -4$, then $-4 < -1$.

- **Transitive Property**
  For any three integers a, b, and c, if $a > b$ and $b > c$, then $a > c$.

  EXAMPLE: If $3 > 2$ and $2 > -3$, then $3 > -3$.

7.3 Operating with Inequalities

- **Adding**
  If $a > b$, then $a + c > b + c$.

  EXAMPLE: If $6 > 4$ and $c = 2$, then $6 + 2 > 4 + 2$.
  Since $8 > 6$, the statement is true.

  If $a < b$, then $a + c < b + c$.

  EXAMPLE: If $-3 < -2$ and $c = -1$, then
  $-3 + (-1) < -2 + (-1)$.
  Since $-4 < -3$, the statement is true.

- **Subtracting**
  If $a > b$, then $a - c > b - c$.

  EXAMPLE: If $6 > 4$ and $c = 2$, then $6 - 2 > 4 - 2$.
  Since $4 > 2$, the statement is true.

  If $a < b$, then $a - c < b - c$.

  EXAMPLE: If $-5 < 2$ and $c = -3$, then
  $-5 - (-3) < 2 - (-3)$.
  Since $-5 - (-3) < 2 - (-3)$
  $\qquad -5 + 3 < 2 + 3$
  $\qquad\qquad -2 < 5$, the statement is true.

- **Multiplying**

  If $a > b$ and $c > 0$, then $ac > bc$.

  EXAMPLE: If $6 > 4$ and $c = 2$, then $6(2) > 4(2)$.
  Since $12 > 8$, the statement is true.

  If $a > b$ and $c < 0$, then $ac < bc$.

  EXAMPLE: If $6 > 4$ and $c = -2$, then $6(-2) < 4(-2)$.
  Since $-12 < -8$, the statement is true.

- **Dividing**

  If $a > b$ and $c > 0$, then $\frac{a}{c} > \frac{b}{c}$.

  EXAMPLE: If $6 > 4$ and $c = 2$, then $\frac{6}{2} > \frac{4}{2}$.
  Since $3 > 2$, the statement is true.

  If $a > b$ and $c < 0$, then $\frac{a}{c} < \frac{b}{c}$.

  EXAMPLE: If $6 > 4$ and $c = -2$, then $-\frac{6}{2} < -\frac{4}{2}$.
  Since $-3 < -2$, the statement is true.

7.4 Solving Inequalities

Inequalities are solved in the same manner as are equations. To solve, get all the variables on one side of the inequality sign and all numbers or constant terms on the other side.

EXAMPLE: For what values of x is $5x > x + 2$ a true statement?

$$5x > x + 2$$

Subtract x from both sides of the inequality.

$$5x - x > x + 2 - x$$
$$4x > 2$$

Now, divide both sides by 4.

$$x > \frac{1}{2}$$

Therefore, $5x > x + 2$ whenever $x > \frac{1}{2}$.

7.5 Graphing Inequalities

The graph of an inequality in one variable is the set of all points corresponding to the numbers in the solution set of the inequality.

EXAMPLE: Graph the solution set of $x > 3$.

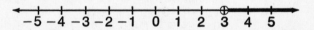

Because 3 is *not* a member of the solution set, it is marked by an open circle. Then every point to the right of 3 is marked with a heavy line.

EXAMPLE: Graph the solution set of $x \le 1$.

Because 1 is included in the solution set, it is marked by a closed circle. Then every point to the left of 1 is marked with a heavy line.

7.6 Compound inequalities

A compound inequality is an expression that combines two inequalities.

EXAMPLE: $-4 < x < 5$ states that $x > -4$ and $x < 5$.

The graph shows the solution set of $x > -4$.

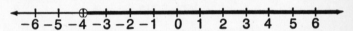

The graph shows the solution set of $x < 5$.

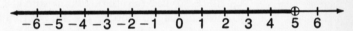

The graph shows the solution set of $-4 < x < 5$.

The graph of $-4 < x < 5$ consists of all points between the point associated with -4 and the point associated with 5.

In a compound inequality the solution must satisfy both inequalities simultaneously.

EXAMPLE: If $2 < 3x - 7 \le 8$, then what values of x will satisfy the condition?
Add 7 to the entire inequality.

$$2 + 7 < 3x - 7 + 7 \le 8 + 7$$
$$9 < 3x \le 15$$

Divide by 3.
$$3 < x \le 5$$

Thus, x can be greater than 3 but less than or equal to 5.

For example, try $x = 4$.

$$2 < 3x - 7 \le 8$$
$$2 \overset{?}{<} 3(4) - 7 \overset{?}{\le} 8$$
$$2 \overset{?}{<} 12 - 7 \overset{?}{\le} 8$$
$$2 < 5 \le 8$$

Since $5 > 2$ and $5 \le 8$, the value $x = 4$ is a member of the solution set.

PROBLEM SOLVING

Although there is no general method for attacking algebra problems, here are some suggestions that should help you in solving verbal problems.

- Read the problem completely and carefully.
- Look for the question in the problem. This usually determines what you are solving for.
- Let x equal the unknown or what you are trying to find.
- Translate the words of the problem, a piece at a time, into an algebraic equation.
- Solve the equation.
- Answer the question.
- Check your answer.

8.1 Number Problems

1. There are two numbers whose sum is 72. One number is three times the other. What are the numbers?

   SOLUTION
   Since one number is three times the other, represent the two numbers in the following way.

   Let n = the smaller number
   $3n$ = the larger number

   Write an equation and solve.
   $$\begin{aligned} n + 3n &= 72 \quad \text{(The sum of the numbers is 72.)} \\ 4n &= 72 \quad \text{(Combine like terms.)} \\ n &= 18 \quad \text{(Divide both sides by 4.)} \\ 3n &= 3(18) = 54 \end{aligned}$$

   Thus, the two numbers are 18 and 54.

   Check
   $$18 + 54 = 72 \ \text{ and } \ 3(18) = 54$$

2. There are two numbers whose sum is 45. Four times the first number is 2 less than three times the second. What are the numbers?

   SOLUTION
   a. two numbers whose sum is 45
   Let n = the first number
   $45 - n$ = the second number

   b. four times the first number: $4n$

   c. 2 less than three times the second: $3(45 - n) - 2$

Write an equation and solve.

$$4n = 3(45 - n) - 2$$
$$4n = 135 - 3n - 2$$
$$7n = 133$$
$$n = 19$$
$$45 - n = 45 - 19 = 26$$

Thus, the two numbers are 19 and 26.

Check

$$19 + 26 = 45 \text{ and } 4(19) = 76$$
$$3(26) - 2 = 78 - 2 = 76$$

8.2 Consecutive Integer Problems

1. The sum of three consecutive integers is 54. Find the numbers.

    SOLUTION
    Let n = 1st consecutive integer
    $n + 1$ = 2nd consecutive integer
    $n + 2$ = 3rd consecutive integer

    Write an equation and solve.
    $$n + (n + 1) + (n + 2) = 54$$
    $$3n + 3 = 54$$
    $$3n = 51$$
    $$n = 17$$
    $$n + 1 = 18$$
    $$n + 2 = 19$$

    Thus, the three consecutive integers are 17, 18, and 19.

    Check
    17, 18, and 19 are consecutive integers and
    17 + 18 + 19 = 54.

2. There are three consecutive even integers. Two times the largest is four times the smallest. What are the integers?

    SOLUTION
    Let n = 1st consecutive even integer
    $n + 2$ = 2nd consecutive even integer
    $n + 4$ = 3rd consecutive even integer

    Write an equation and solve.
    $$2(n + 4) = 4(n)$$
    $$2n + 8 = 4n$$
    $$8 = 2n$$
    $$4 = n$$
    $$6 = n + 2$$
    $$8 = n + 4$$

    Thus, the three consecutive even integers are 4, 6, and 8.

Check
4, 6, and 8 are consecutive even integers and two times the largest (2 · 8) is four times the smallest (4 · 4). Thus, 2 · 8 = 4 · 4 or 16 = 16.

8.3 Rate, Time, and Distance Problems

1. A train averaging 50 mph leaves Boston at 1 P.M. for New York, 330 miles away. At the same time, a second train leaves New York headed for Boston, traveling on the same tracks at an average rate of 60 mph. At what time will the two trains meet?

   SOLUTION
   First, draw a diagram to show their movement.

   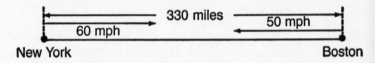

   New York   Boston

   Remember: rate × time = distance or $r \times t = d$.

   Let t = time in hours for the two trains to meet
   $50t$ = distance the train from Boston travels
   $60t$ = distance the train from New York travels

   Since the total distance traveled by both trains is 330 miles, write an equation and solve.
   $$50t + 60t = 330$$
   $$110t = 330$$
   $$t = 3$$

   Thus, the two trains will meet in 3 hours or at 4 P.M.

   Check
   The train from Boston travels 50(3) = 150 miles.
   The train from New York travels 60(3) = 180 miles.
   Thus, 150 + 180 = 330 or 330 miles.

2. Two planes leave a city at 9 A.M. One travels due north at 600 mph and the other due south at 450 mph. At what time will they be 1575 miles apart?

   SOLUTION
   First, draw a diagram to show their movement.

   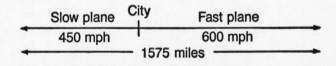

   Let t = time in hours for the planes to fly
   1575 miles apart

$450t =$ distance the slow plane traveled
$600t =$ distance the fast plane traveled

Since the total distance traveled is 1575 miles, write an equation and solve.

$$450t + 600t = 1575$$
$$1050t = 1575$$
$$t = \frac{1575}{1050}$$
$$t = 1\tfrac{1}{2}$$

Thus, the two planes will be 1575 miles apart in $1\tfrac{1}{2}$ hours or at 10:30 A.M.

Check
The slow plane travels $450(1\tfrac{1}{2})$ or 675 miles.

The fast plane travels $600(1\tfrac{1}{2})$ or 900 miles.

Thus, $675 + 900 = 1575$ or 1575 miles.

3. Sarah left her home at 9 A.M. traveling in her car at 32 mph. Two hours later, her brother started after her on the same road, traveling in his car at 48 mph. At what time did her brother overtake Sarah?

SOLUTION
Draw a diagram to show their movement.

Let $t =$ time in hours for her brother to overtake Sarah

Since Sarah started 2 hours earlier than her brother, she traveled 2 hours longer than her brother.

Let
$t+2 =$ time in hours Sarah traveled
$32(t+2) =$ distance Sarah traveled
$48t =$ distance her brother traveled

They travel the same distance so set the distances equal to each other. Then solve the equation.

$$32(t + 2) = 48t$$
$$32t + 64 = 48t$$
$$64 = 16t$$
$$4 = t$$

Thus, Sarah's brother overtook her in 4 hours or at 3 P.M.

Check
Sarah traveled $32(4 + 2)$ or $32 \times 6 = 192$ miles.
Her brother traveled $48(4)$ or 192 miles

4. In his motorboat, a man starts down a river whose current flows at 5 mph. The man finds that he can go downstream in 1 hour less time than it takes him to go upstream the same distance. How fast can he travel in still water if it takes him 2 hours to travel upstream the given distance?

SOLUTION
First, draw a diagram to show his movement.

	Current	
Upstream	5 mph	Downstream
$t = 2h$		$t = 1h$

Let

r = rate of boat in mph in still water
$r + 5$ = rate of boat in mph downstream
$r - 5$ = rate of boat in mph upstream
$1(r + 5)$ = distance boat traveled downstream
$2(r - 5)$ = distance boat traveled upstream

He travels the same distances, so write an equation and solve.

$$1(r + 5) = 2(r - 5)$$
$$r + 5 = 2r - 10$$
$$15 = r$$

Thus, the motorboat travels 15 mph in still water.

Check
The rate of the motorboat traveling downstream is $15 + 5 = 20$ mph.
The rate of the motorboat traveling upstream is $15 - 5 = 10$ mph.
The distance traveled downstream is $1(20) = 20$ miles.
The distance traveled upstream is $2(10) = 20$ miles.

8.4 Mixture Problems

1. A farmer wants to mix milk containing 6% butterfat with 2 quarts of cream that is 15% butterfat in order to obtain a mixture that is 12% butterfat. How much milk containing 6% butterfat must he use?

SOLUTION
Draw a diagram to show the three solutions.
Let b = number of quarts of milk containing 6% butterfat

b qt		2 qt		$(b + 2)$qt
6%	+	15%	=	12%

Represent the amount of butterfat in each.
$$0.06b + 0.15(2) = 0.12(b + 2)$$
Multiply by 100.
$$6b + 15(2) = 12(b + 2)$$
$$6b + 30 = 12b + 24$$
$$6 = 6b$$
$$1 = b$$

Thus, he must use 1 quart of the milk containing 6% butterfat.

Check
1 qt containing 6% butterfat has 0.06 qt of butterfat.
2 qt containing 15% butterfat has 0.3 qt of butterfat.
3 qt containing 12% butterfat has 0.36 qt of butterfat.
$$0.06 + 0.3 = 0.36$$
$$0.36 = 0.36$$

2. A store owner has 12 pounds of pasta worth 70 cents a pound. She wants to mix it with pasta worth 45 cents a pound so that the total mixture can be sold for 55 cents a pound without any gain or loss. How much of the 45-cent pasta must she use?

SOLUTION
Draw a diagram to show the three types of pasta.
Let x = the number of pounds of the 45-cent pasta

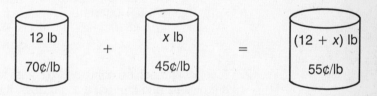

Find the cost, in cents, of each pasta.
$$70(12) + 45(x) = 55(12 + x)$$
$$840 + 45x = 660 + 55x$$
$$180 = 10x$$
$$18 = x$$

Thus, she must use 18 pounds of the 45-cent pasta.

Check
The cost of the 70-cent pasta is $70(12) = 840$¢ or $8.40.
The cost of the 45-cent pasta is $45(18) = 810$¢ or $8.10.
The cost of the 55-cent pasta is $55(30) = 1650$¢ or $16.50.
$$\$8.10 + \$8.40 = \$16.50$$
$$\$16.50 = \$16.50$$

8.5 Coin Problems

1. Mary collected $16.80 in half-dollars, quarters, and dimes. There were twice as many quarters as half-dollars, and twice as many dimes as quarters. How many of each kind of coin did Mary collect?

    SOLUTION

    Let
    $$x = \text{the number of half-dollars}$$
    $$2x = \text{the number of quarters}$$
    $$2(2x) = \text{the number of dimes}$$
    $$50x = \text{value in cents of half-dollars}$$
    $$25(2x) = \text{value in cents of quarters}$$
    $$10(4x) = \text{value in cents of dimes}$$

    Write an equation and solve.
    $$50x + 25(2x) + 10(4x) = 1680 \quad (\$16.80 = 1680 \text{ cents})$$
    $$50x + 50x + 40x = 1680$$
    $$140x = 1680$$
    $$x = 12$$
    $$2x = 24$$
    $$4x = 48$$

    Thus, Mary collected 12 half-dollars, 24 quarters, and 48 dimes.

    Check

12 half-dollars	=	$ 6.00
24 quarters	=	6.00
48 dimes	=	+ 4.80
		$16.80

2. A vending machine contains 20 coins; some of the coins are nickels and the rest are quarters. If the value of the coins is $4.40, find the number of coins of each kind.

    SOLUTION

    Let
    $$x = \text{the number of nickels}$$
    $$20 - x = \text{the number of quarters}$$
    $$5x = \text{value in cents of nickels}$$
    $$25(20 - x) = \text{value in cents of quarters}$$

    Write an equation and solve.
    $$5x + 25(20 - x) = 440 \quad (\$4.40 = 440 \text{ cents})$$
    $$5x + 500 - 25x = 440$$
    $$-20x = -60$$
    $$x = 3$$
    $$20 - x = 17$$

    Thus, there are 3 nickels and 17 quarters.

    Check

17 quarters	=	$4.25
3 nickels	=	+ .15
		$4.40

8.6 Age Problems

1. Pat's father is now 3 times as old as Pat. In 10 years, he will be twice as old as Pat will be then. What are their present ages?

SOLUTION

Let
$$x = \text{the present age of Pat}$$
$$3x = \text{the present age of Pat's father}$$
$$x + 10 = \text{Pat's age in 10 years from now}$$
$$3x + 10 = \text{Pat's father's age in 10 years from now}$$

Since Pat's father's age 10 years from now will be twice Pat's age then, write an equation and solve.
$$3x + 10 = 2(x + 10)$$
$$3x + 10 = 2x + 20$$
$$x = 10$$
$$3x = 30$$

Thus, Pat is 10 years old and her father is 30.

Check
In 10 years, Pat will be 20 years old. In 10 years, Pat's father will be 40 years old. Therefore, Pat's father will be twice Pat's age then.

2. Jane is twice as old as Renee. If 3 is subtracted from Renee's age and 9 is added to Jane's age, Jane will then be 3 times as old as Renee. Find their ages.

SOLUTION

Let
$$a = \text{Renee's age now}$$
$$2a = \text{Jane's age now}$$
$$a - 3 = \text{3 subtracted from Renee's age}$$
$$2a + 9 = \text{9 added to Jane's age}$$

Then,
$$2a + 9 = 3(a - 3)$$
$$2a + 9 = 3a - 9$$
$$18 = a$$
$$36 = 2a$$

Thus, Renee is 18 and Jane is 36.

Check
Three subtracted from Renee's age is $18 - 3 = 15$. Nine added to Jane's age is $36 + 9 = 45$. Since $45 = 3(15)$, Jane's age is 3 times Renee's age.

8.7 Finance Problems

1. Florence invested $8000. Part of it she put in the bank at 6% interest. The remainder she put in a pension plan which paid a 4% yearly return. Her total annual income from the investments is $380. How much has she invested at each rate?

Use the formula $i = p \times r \times t$, where
i = interest, income, or return
p = principal or amount of money invested
r = rate of interest or percent
t = number of years for which the principal is invested

Let y = amount in dollars invested at 6%
$8000 - y$ = amount in dollars invested at 4%

To find the interest for each investment, use the formula
$$i = p \times r \times t$$
Since we are speaking of annual income, t = 1 year.

So, $0.06y$ = interest from bank investment
$0.04(8000 - y)$ = interest from pension plan

Since the total annual income from the investments is $380, write an equation and solve.
$$0.06y + 0.04(8000 - y) = 380$$
Multiply by 100.
$$6y + 4(8000 - y) = 38000$$
$$6y + 32000 - 4y = 38000$$
$$2y = 6000$$
$$y = 3000$$
$$8000 - y = 5000$$

Thus, $3000 was invested in the bank and $5000 was invested in the pension plan.

Check
$3000 invested at 6% will earn 0.06(3000) or $180.
$5000 invested at 4% will earn 0.04(5000) or $200.
The total annual income from the investments is
$$\$180 + \$200 = \$380$$

2. A store bought 500 jackets, part at $70 each and the rest at $90 each. If the total cost of the jackets was $37,800, how many jackets were purchased at each price?

SOLUTION
Let x = number of jackets at $70 each
$500 - x$ = number of jackets at $90 each
$70x$ = cost of the $70 jackets
$90(500 - x)$ = cost of the $90 jackets

Then, $70x + 90(500 - x) = 37800$
$$70x + 45000 - 90x = 37800$$
$$-20x = -7200$$
$$x = 360$$
$$500 - x = 140$$

Thus, 360 jackets were purchased at $70 each and 140 jackets were purchased at $90 each.

Check
$$140 + 360 = 500$$
cost of 360 jackets at $70 each = $25,200
cost of 140 jackets at $90 each = + 12,600
$$\$37,800$$

8.8 Work Problems

1. Eve can address a box of envelopes in 30 minutes. Her sister, May, can address a box of envelopes in 1 hour. How long would it take both girls working together to address a box of envelopes?

    SOLUTION
    You need to work with the same unit of time, so change 1 hour to 60 minutes.
    Let x = the number of minutes to address a box of envelopes together

    Set up the following chart:

	Time working alone (in minutes)	Part of job done in 1 minute	Part of job done working together
Eve	30	$\frac{1}{30}$	$x\left(\frac{1}{30}\right) = \frac{x}{30}$
May	60	$\frac{1}{60}$	$x\left(\frac{1}{60}\right) = \frac{x}{60}$

    If the complete job is represented by 1, then the sum of the parts of the job each does working together will equal 1.
    $$\frac{x}{30} + \frac{x}{60} = 1$$
    Multiply both sides of the equation by 60.
    $$60\left(\frac{x}{30} + \frac{x}{60}\right) = 60(1)$$
    $$2x + x = 60$$
    $$3x = 60$$
    $$x = 20$$

    Thus, it would take 20 minutes for both girls working together to address a box of envelopes.

    Check
    Eve will complete $\frac{20}{30}$ or $\frac{2}{3}$ of the job in 20 minutes.

    May will complete $\frac{20}{60}$ or $\frac{1}{3}$ of the job in 20 minutes.
    $$\frac{2}{3} + \frac{1}{3} = 1$$

2. When 2 intake pipes are opened, a tank can be filled in 10 minutes. One of the pipes alone can fill the tank in 15 minutes. How long would it take the second pipe alone to fill the tank?

Let x = the number of minutes for the second pipe alone to fill the tank

Set up the following chart:

	Time working alone (in minutes)	Part filled in 1 minute	Part filled in 10 minutes
1st pipe	15	$\frac{1}{15}$	$10\left(\frac{1}{15}\right) = \frac{2}{3}$
2nd pipe	x	$\frac{1}{x}$	$10\left(\frac{1}{x}\right) = \frac{10}{x}$

Then, $\qquad\qquad\qquad \frac{2}{3} + \frac{10}{x} = 1$

Multiply both sides of the equation by $3x$.

$$3x\left(\frac{2}{3} + \frac{10}{x}\right) = 3x(1)$$
$$2x + 30 = 3x$$
$$30 = x$$

Thus, the second pipe working alone will fill the tank in 30 minutes.

Check

The first pipe will fill $\frac{10}{15}$ or $\frac{2}{3}$ of the tank in 10 minutes.

The second pipe will fill $\frac{10}{30}$ or $\frac{1}{3}$ of the tank in 10 minutes.

$$\frac{2}{3} + \frac{1}{3} = 1$$

8.9 Digit Problems

1. The tens digit of a 2-digit number is 1 more than twice the units digit. The sum of the digits is 7. Find the number.

   SOLUTION
   Let $\qquad u$ = units digit
   $\qquad 2u + 1$ = tens digit

   Then, $\qquad\qquad u + (2u + 1) = 7$
   $$3u + 1 = 7$$
   $$3u = 6$$
   $$u = 2$$
   $$2u + 1 = 5$$

   Thus, using the values above for the units and tens digits, the number is written as 10 (tens digit) + units digit, or $10(5) + 2 = 52$.

   Check
   The tens digit (5) is 1 more than twice the units digit (2), and $5 + 2 = 7$.

2. The sum of the digits of a 2-digit number is 8. The number exceeds the sum of its digits by 9. Find the number.

SOLUTION
Remember, the value of a digit depends on its place in the number. For example, $347 = 3(100) + 4(10) + 7(1)$.

Let $u =$ units digit
$t =$ tens digit
$10t + u =$ the number

Then, $$t + u = 8$$
$$10t + u = (t + u) + 9$$
Simplify the second equation.
$$10t + u = t + u + 9$$
$$9t = 9$$
$$t = 1$$
Substitute 1 for t in $t + u = 8$.
$$1 + u = 8$$
$$u = 7$$

Thus, $10t + u = 10(1) + 7 = 17$.

Check
The sum of the digits is $1 + 7 = 8$, and 17 is 9 more than this sum.

8.10 Geometric Problems

1. The length of a rectangle is 6 times its width. The perimeter is 42 feet. Find the dimensions of the rectangle.

SOLUTION
Let $w =$ the number of feet in the width
$6w =$ the number of feet in the length

Draw a diagram to illustrate the problem.

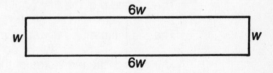

The perimeter of a rectangle is the sum of the measures of its four sides, so
$$w + 6w + w + 6w = 42$$
$$14w = 42$$
$$w = 3$$
$$6w = 18$$

Thus, the width of the rectangle is 3 feet and the length is 18 feet.

Check
$$18 = 6(3) \text{ and } 3 + 18 + 3 + 18 = 42$$

2. The measure of the first angle of a triangle is twice the measure of the second, and the measure of the third is 30 degrees more than that of the first. Find the degree measure of each angle of the triangle.

SOLUTION

Let x = number of degrees in the measure of the second angle

$2x$ = number of degrees in the measure of the first angle

$2x + 30$ = number of degrees in the measure of the third angle

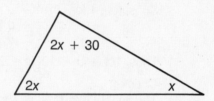

Since the sum of the degree measures of the three angles of any triangle is 180, write an equation and solve.
$$x + 2x + 2x + 30 = 180$$
$$5x + 30 = 180$$
$$5x = 150$$
$$x = 30$$
$$2x = 60$$
$$2x + 30 = 90$$

Thus, the measures of the three angles are 30°, 60°, and 90°.

Check
The measure of the first angle is twice the second.
$$60° = 2(30°)$$
The measure of the third angle is 30° more than the first.
$$90° = 60° + 30°$$
The sum of the measures of the angles is 180°.
$$30° + 60° + 90° = 180°$$

8.11 Problems Leading to Quadratic Equations

1. Two consecutive positive odd numbers have a product of 675. What are the numbers?

SOLUTION

Let x = the first consecutive positive odd number
$x + 2$ = the second consecutive positive odd number

Since the product of the two numbers is 675, write an equation and solve.

$$x(x + 2) = 675$$
$$x^2 + 2x = 675$$
$$x^2 + 2x - 675 = 0$$
$$(x + 27)(x - 25) = 0$$
$$x + 27 = 0 \quad \text{or} \quad x - 25 = 0$$
$$x = -27 \qquad\qquad x = 25$$
$$\text{(Reject)} \qquad x + 2 = 27$$

Thus, the two consecutive positive odd numbers are 25 and 27.

Check
25 and 27 are consecutive positive odd numbers and $25(27) = 675$.

2. Gerry traveled 90 miles at an average rate of speed. If she had increased her speed 12 mph, she could have covered the same distance in 2 hours less time. How fast did she travel?

SOLUTION

Let x = rate in mph before increase
$x + 12$ = rate in mph after increase

	Rate	Time	Distance
Before	x	$\dfrac{90}{x}$	90
After	$x + 12$	$\dfrac{90}{x + 12}$	90

Since the time after the increase is 2 hours less than the time before, the equation is

$$\frac{90}{x + 12} = \frac{90}{x} - 2$$

Multiply by the LCD, $x(x + 12)$.

$$x(x + 12)\left(\frac{90}{x + 12}\right) = x(x + 12)\left(\frac{90}{x} - 2\right)$$
$$90x = 90(x + 12) - 2(x)(x + 12)$$
$$90x = 90x + 1080 - 2x^2 - 24x$$
$$0 = 1080 - 2x^2 - 24x$$

$$2x^2 + 24x - 1080 = 0$$

Simplify by dividing by 2.
$$x^2 + 12x - 540 = 0$$
$$(x + 30)(x - 18) = 0$$

$x + 30 = 0$	or	$x - 18 = 0$
$x = -30$		$x = 18$
(Reject)		$x + 12 = 30$

Thus, she traveled at 18 mph.

Check
At 18 mph, a trip of 90 miles would take $\frac{90}{18}$ or 5 hours.

If the speed is increased by 12 mph, a trip of 90 miles would take $\frac{90}{30}$ or 3 hours.

The trip took her 5 hours. If she had incresed her speed, the trip would have taken 2 hours less, or 3 hours.

Part Three

Practice Tests in Specific Algebra Areas

This section has Practice Tests for each of the eight areas found in the Algebra Refresher Section.

Use the appropriate Answer Sheet on pages 76-79 to record your answers.

After you have completed each test, you can check your answers using the Answer Keys on pages 96-98. Each answer is referenced to the appropriate Algebra Refresher Section. The references, in parentheses, follow the answer and are in the same form as in the Answer Key to the Diagnostic Tests.

The solutions, with error analysis for each problem, begin on page 99.

Areas	Pages		
	Answer Sheet	Test	Answer Key
Integers	76	80	96
Algebraic Expressions	76	82	96
Factoring	77	84	97
Equations	77	86	97
Ratio and Proportion	78	88	97
Probability	78	90	98
Inequalities	79	92	98
Problem Solving	79	94	98

Answer Sheets

Practice Tests

INTEGERS

1. Ⓐ Ⓑ Ⓒ Ⓓ
2. Ⓐ Ⓑ Ⓒ Ⓓ
3. Ⓐ Ⓑ Ⓒ Ⓓ
4. Ⓐ Ⓑ Ⓒ Ⓓ
5. Ⓐ Ⓑ Ⓒ Ⓓ
6. Ⓐ Ⓑ Ⓒ Ⓓ
7. Ⓐ Ⓑ Ⓒ Ⓓ
8. Ⓐ Ⓑ Ⓒ Ⓓ
9. Ⓐ Ⓑ Ⓒ Ⓓ
10. Ⓐ Ⓑ Ⓒ Ⓓ

11. Ⓐ Ⓑ Ⓒ Ⓓ
12. Ⓐ Ⓑ Ⓒ Ⓓ
13. Ⓐ Ⓑ Ⓒ Ⓓ
14. Ⓐ Ⓑ Ⓒ Ⓓ
15. Ⓐ Ⓑ Ⓒ Ⓓ
16. Ⓐ Ⓑ Ⓒ Ⓓ
17. Ⓐ Ⓑ Ⓒ Ⓓ
18. Ⓐ Ⓑ Ⓒ Ⓓ
19. Ⓐ Ⓑ Ⓒ Ⓓ
20. Ⓐ Ⓑ Ⓒ Ⓓ

ALGEBRAIC EXPRESSIONS

1. Ⓐ Ⓑ Ⓒ Ⓓ
2. Ⓐ Ⓑ Ⓒ Ⓓ
3. Ⓐ Ⓑ Ⓒ Ⓓ
4. Ⓐ Ⓑ Ⓒ Ⓓ
5. Ⓐ Ⓑ Ⓒ Ⓓ
6. Ⓐ Ⓑ Ⓒ Ⓓ
7. Ⓐ Ⓑ Ⓒ Ⓓ
8. Ⓐ Ⓑ Ⓒ Ⓓ
9. Ⓐ Ⓑ Ⓒ Ⓓ
10. Ⓐ Ⓑ Ⓒ Ⓓ

11. Ⓐ Ⓑ Ⓒ Ⓓ
12. Ⓐ Ⓑ Ⓒ Ⓓ
13. Ⓐ Ⓑ Ⓒ Ⓓ
14. Ⓐ Ⓑ Ⓒ Ⓓ
15. Ⓐ Ⓑ Ⓒ Ⓓ
16. Ⓐ Ⓑ Ⓒ Ⓓ
17. Ⓐ Ⓑ Ⓒ Ⓓ
18. Ⓐ Ⓑ Ⓒ Ⓓ
19. Ⓐ Ⓑ Ⓒ Ⓓ
20. Ⓐ Ⓑ Ⓒ Ⓓ

FACTORING

1. Ⓐ Ⓑ Ⓒ Ⓓ
2. Ⓐ Ⓑ Ⓒ Ⓓ
3. Ⓐ Ⓑ Ⓒ Ⓓ
4. Ⓐ Ⓑ Ⓒ Ⓓ
5. Ⓐ Ⓑ Ⓒ Ⓓ
6. Ⓐ Ⓑ Ⓒ Ⓓ
7. Ⓐ Ⓑ Ⓒ Ⓓ
8. Ⓐ Ⓑ Ⓒ Ⓓ
9. Ⓐ Ⓑ Ⓒ Ⓓ
10. Ⓐ Ⓑ Ⓒ Ⓓ

11. Ⓐ Ⓑ Ⓒ Ⓓ
12. Ⓐ Ⓑ Ⓒ Ⓓ
13. Ⓐ Ⓑ Ⓒ Ⓓ
14. Ⓐ Ⓑ Ⓒ Ⓓ
15. Ⓐ Ⓑ Ⓒ Ⓓ
16. Ⓐ Ⓑ Ⓒ Ⓓ
17. Ⓐ Ⓑ Ⓒ Ⓓ
18. Ⓐ Ⓑ Ⓒ Ⓓ
19. Ⓐ Ⓑ Ⓒ Ⓓ
20. Ⓐ Ⓑ Ⓒ Ⓓ

EQUATIONS

1. Ⓐ Ⓑ Ⓒ Ⓓ
2. Ⓐ Ⓑ Ⓒ Ⓓ
3. Ⓐ Ⓑ Ⓒ Ⓓ
4. Ⓐ Ⓑ Ⓒ Ⓓ
5. Ⓐ Ⓑ Ⓒ Ⓓ
6. Ⓐ Ⓑ Ⓒ Ⓓ
7. Ⓐ Ⓑ Ⓒ Ⓓ
8. Ⓐ Ⓑ Ⓒ Ⓓ
9. Ⓐ Ⓑ Ⓒ Ⓓ
10. Ⓐ Ⓑ Ⓒ Ⓓ

11. Ⓐ Ⓑ Ⓒ Ⓓ
12. Ⓐ Ⓑ Ⓒ Ⓓ
13. Ⓐ Ⓑ Ⓒ Ⓓ
14. Ⓐ Ⓑ Ⓒ Ⓓ
15. Ⓐ Ⓑ Ⓒ Ⓓ
16. Ⓐ Ⓑ Ⓒ Ⓓ
17. Ⓐ Ⓑ Ⓒ Ⓓ
18. Ⓐ Ⓑ Ⓒ Ⓓ
19. Ⓐ Ⓑ Ⓒ Ⓓ
20. Ⓐ Ⓑ Ⓒ Ⓓ

RATIO AND PROPORTION

1. Ⓐ Ⓑ Ⓒ Ⓓ
2. Ⓐ Ⓑ Ⓒ Ⓓ
3. Ⓐ Ⓑ Ⓒ Ⓓ
4. Ⓐ Ⓑ Ⓒ Ⓓ
5. Ⓐ Ⓑ Ⓒ Ⓓ
6. Ⓐ Ⓑ Ⓒ Ⓓ
7. Ⓐ Ⓑ Ⓒ Ⓓ
8. Ⓐ Ⓑ Ⓒ Ⓓ
9. Ⓐ Ⓑ Ⓒ Ⓓ
10. Ⓐ Ⓑ Ⓒ Ⓓ

11. Ⓐ Ⓑ Ⓒ Ⓓ
12. Ⓐ Ⓑ Ⓒ Ⓓ
13. Ⓐ Ⓑ Ⓒ Ⓓ
14. Ⓐ Ⓑ Ⓒ Ⓓ
15. Ⓐ Ⓑ Ⓒ Ⓓ
16. Ⓐ Ⓑ Ⓒ Ⓓ
17. Ⓐ Ⓑ Ⓒ Ⓓ
18. Ⓐ Ⓑ Ⓒ Ⓓ
19. Ⓐ Ⓑ Ⓒ Ⓓ
20. Ⓐ Ⓑ Ⓒ Ⓓ

PROBABILITY

1. Ⓐ Ⓑ Ⓒ Ⓓ
2. Ⓐ Ⓑ Ⓒ Ⓓ
3. Ⓐ Ⓑ Ⓒ Ⓓ
4. Ⓐ Ⓑ Ⓒ Ⓓ
5. Ⓐ Ⓑ Ⓒ Ⓓ
6. Ⓐ Ⓑ Ⓒ Ⓓ
7. Ⓐ Ⓑ Ⓒ Ⓓ
8. Ⓐ Ⓑ Ⓒ Ⓓ
9. Ⓐ Ⓑ Ⓒ Ⓓ
10. Ⓐ Ⓑ Ⓒ Ⓓ

11. Ⓐ Ⓑ Ⓒ Ⓓ
12. Ⓐ Ⓑ Ⓒ Ⓓ
13. Ⓐ Ⓑ Ⓒ Ⓓ
14. Ⓐ Ⓑ Ⓒ Ⓓ
15. Ⓐ Ⓑ Ⓒ Ⓓ
16. Ⓐ Ⓑ Ⓒ Ⓓ
17. Ⓐ Ⓑ Ⓒ Ⓓ
18. Ⓐ Ⓑ Ⓒ Ⓓ
19. Ⓐ Ⓑ Ⓒ Ⓓ
20. Ⓐ Ⓑ Ⓒ Ⓓ

INEQUALITIES

1. (A) (B) (C) (D)
2. (A) (B) (C) (D)
3. (A) (B) (C) (D)
4. (A) (B) (C) (D)
5. (A) (B) (C) (D)
6. (A) (B) (C) (D)
7. (A) (B) (C) (D)
8. (A) (B) (C) (D)
9. (A) (B) (C) (D)
10. (A) (B) (C) (D)

11. (A) (B) (C) (D)
12. (A) (B) (C) (D)
13. (A) (B) (C) (D)
14. (A) (B) (C) (D)
15. (A) (B) (C) (D)
16. (A) (B) (C) (D)
17. (A) (B) (C) (D)
18. (A) (B) (C) (D)
19. (A) (B) (C) (D)
20. (A) (B) (C) (D)

PROBLEM SOLVING

1. (A) (B) (C) (D)
2. (A) (B) (C) (D)
3. (A) (B) (C) (D)
4. (A) (B) (C) (D)
5. (A) (B) (C) (D)
6. (A) (B) (C) (D)
7. (A) (B) (C) (D)
8. (A) (B) (C) (D)
9. (A) (B) (C) (D)
10. (A) (B) (C) (D)

11. (A) (B) (C) (D)
12. (A) (B) (C) (D)
13. (A) (B) (C) (D)
14. (A) (B) (C) (D)
15. (A) (B) (C) (D)
16. (A) (B) (C) (D)
17. (A) (B) (C) (D)
18. (A) (B) (C) (D)
19. (A) (B) (C) (D)
20. (A) (B) (C) (D)

Algebra Practice Tests

INTEGERS

1. Which of the following conditions will make $x + y$ a negative number?

(A) $x = y$ (B) $y > x$ (C) $y < -x$ (D) $x < 0$

2. $1 - 3$ equals

(A) -4 (B) -2 (C) $+4$ (D) $+2$

3. If x and y are positive integers and if $\frac{x}{y} = 1$ and $(x + y)^2 = z$, which of the following *can* equal z?

(A) 5   (B) 9   (C) 16   (D) 25

4. The sum of 3, -4, and y is equal to the sum of y and

(A) -1 (B) -7 (C) $+7$ (D) $y - 1$

5. $(-1)(-2)(-3)(+4) =$

(A) -10 (B) $+24$ (C) -24 (D) -36

6. Of the following values of N, $(-\frac{1}{2})^N$ will have the least value when $N =$

(A) 3   (B) 4   (C) 5   (D) 6

7. If x and y are integers and if $x - y < x + y$, which of the following must be true?

(A) $y > 0$ (B) $x > 0$ (C) $x = y$ (D) $x > y$

8. The value of $|-5| - |2|$ is

(A) -7 (B) -3 (C) $+3$ (D) $+7$

9. Which of the following must be positive?

I. The sum of two positive numbers
II. The product of two negative numbers
III. The quotient of two positive numbers

(A) I only   (B) I and II only
(C) II and III only   (D) I, II, and III

10. $(-2) - (-5) =$

(A) -7 (B) -3 (C) $+3$ (D) $+7$

11. $(-5) + (-2) =$

(A) -7 (B) -3 (C) $+3$ (D) $+7$

12. $[(-15) \div (-3)] + (-5) =$

(A) -10 (B) 0 (C) 7 (D) 25

13. Which of the following is equal to $\left(\frac{1}{2}\right) \div \left(-\frac{7}{8}\right)$?

(A) $-\frac{4}{7}$ (B) $-\frac{7}{16}$ (C) $-1\frac{3}{4}$ (D) $-2\frac{2}{7}$

14. The expression $7 - [(-8) + (-2)] =$

(A) -3 (B) -1 (C) 13 (D) 17

15. The integers $-2, -7, 5,$ and -5, written in order from least to greatest, are

(A) $-2, -5, -7, 5$ (B) $-5, -7, -2, 5$
(C) $-7, -5, -2, 5$ (D) $-7, -2, -5, 5$

16. $\left| \frac{(-18) + (-2)}{(+7) + (-2)} \right| =$

(A) -4 (B) $2\frac{2}{9}$ (C) $3\frac{1}{5}$ (D) 4

17. All of the following are equal to $\frac{^-3}{6}$ EXCEPT

(A) $\frac{^-1}{2}$ (B) $\frac{1}{^-2}$ (C) $-\frac{1}{2}$ (D) $-\frac{^-1}{2}$

18. Which of the following conditions will make $r - s$ a negative number?

(A) $s > r$ (B) $s < r$ (C) $s > 0$ (D) $r = s$

19. How many integers are both greater than the integer $n - 1$ and less than the integer n?

(A) 0 (B) 1 (C) n (D) $n - 1$

20. If $m \times n = p$ and $p \neq 0$, where $m, n,$ and p are integers, which of the following must be false?

(A) $p \div m = n$ (B) $n \times m = p$
(C) $m = 0$ (D) $p \div n = m$

ALGEBRAIC EXPRESSIONS

1. $5x^3 + 2y^3 + 3y^3 =$

    (A) $10x^3y^3$ (B) $5x^3 + 5y^3$
    (C) $5x^3 + 5y^6$ (D) $10x^3y^6$

2. The product of $x + 1$ and $3x + 1$ is

    (A) $3x^2 + 4x + 1$ (B) $3x^2 + 3x + 1$
    (C) $3x^2 + 4x + 2$ (D) $4x^2 + 4x + 1$

3. If $a = 1$ and $b = 2$, the value of $3a^3b^2$ is

    (A) 12   (B) 36   (C) 108   (D) 2916

4. If $3x^2 + 4x - 3$ is subtracted from $5x^2 - 2x + 3$, the result is

    (A) $8x^2 + 2x$ (B) $2x^2 - 6x + 6$
    (C) $-2x^2 + 6x - 6$ (D) $2x^2 + 2x$

5. The term which is equivalent to $\frac{9}{y} - \frac{3}{y}$ is

    (A) 6   (B) $6y$ (C) $\frac{6}{y}$ (D) $-\frac{6}{y}$

6. $(5z^2)(4z^3) =$

    (A) $9z^6$ (B) $20z^6$ (C) $20z^5$ (D) $9z^5$

7. The fraction $\frac{8x^4y^3}{2xy^3}$ written in simplest form is

    (A) $6x^3$ (B) $4x^3$ (C) $4x^4$ (D) 4^4

8. If $n - 2$ represents an even integer, the next larger even integer is

    (A) $n - 4$ (B) $n - 1$ (C) n (D) $n + 2$

9. The quotient of $4n^2 - 7n + 3$ and $n - 1$ is

    (A) $4n - 3$ (B) $4n^2 - 6n + 2$
    (C) $4n^3 - 11n^2 + 10n - 3$ (D) $4n - 11 - \frac{8}{n - 1}$

10. The sum of $\frac{x + 1}{2}$ and $\frac{x}{3}$ is

    (A) $\frac{2x + 1}{5}$ (B) $\frac{5x + 1}{6}$ (C) $\frac{8x}{6}$ (D) $\frac{5x + 3}{6}$

11. $\sqrt[3]{27} + \sqrt[5]{32} =$

(A) $\sqrt[8]{59}$ (B) $3\sqrt{3} + 25$
(C) 5   (D) 6

12. If $12x^4 - 3x^3 + 6x^2$ is divided by $3x^2$, the quotient is

(A) $5x^2$ (B) $12x^2 - x + 2$
(C) $4x^2 - 3x + 2$ (D) $4x^2 - x + 2$

13. A number, n, is multiplied by 3. If 19 is subtracted from this expression, the result would be

(A) $\frac{n}{3} - 19$ (B) $3n - 19$ (C) $19 - 3n$ (D) $-16n$

14. $(2x^3)^3 =$

(A) $6x^9$ (B) $6x^{27}$ (C) $8x^{27}$ (D) $8x^9$

15. $(a - b)(c + 2d) =$

(A) $ac + 2ad - bc - 2bd$ (B) $ac + 2ad + bc + 2bd$
(C) $3abcd$ (D) $ac - 2bd$

16. If $x = 3$ and $y = 2$, the value of $(xy)^2$ is

(A) -36 (B) 1   (C) 12   (D) 36

17. If $x * y = \frac{1}{x^2} + y^2$, then which of the following is equal to 1?

(A) $-1 * -1$ (B) $1 * 1$ (C) $1 * 0$ (D) $-1 * 1$

18. What is the result when $5 - 3x$ is subtracted from the sum of $2 + 3x$ and $3x^2 - 3x + 4$?

(A) $3x^2 - 3x + 1$ (B) $3x^2 + 3x + 1$
(C) $3x^2 - 3x + 11$ (D) $-3x^2 - 3x - 1$

19. For all real numbers a and b, where $a \neq 0, a \oplus b = \frac{b + 1}{a}$. Then, $(2 \oplus 3) \oplus 1 =$

(A) $\frac{5}{6}$ (B) 1   (C) 2   (D) 3

20. If $r * s = \frac{r + s}{2} - 1$, then which of the following is equal to 0?

(A) $r * 0$ (B) $s * 0$ (C) $r * -r$ (D) $1 * 1$

FACTORING

1. The greatest common factor of $3x^2y + 6x$ is

   (A) 3   (B) x (C) $3x$ (D) $3xy$

2. Factor $x^2 - 49$.

   (A) $x(x - 49)$ (B) $(x - 7)(x - 7)$
   (C) $(x^2 - 7)(x^2 + 7)$ (D) $(x + 7)(x - 7)$

3. The prime factorization of 72 is

   (A) 1×72 (B) $2^3 \times 3^2$
   (C) $2 \times 3^2 \times 4$ (D) $2 \times 3 \times 12$

4. Factor $6a - 9$.

   (A) $2(3a - 9)$ (B) $3(2a - 3)$
   (C) $6(a - 9)$ (D) $1(6a - 9)$

5. If $x - 3$ is a factor of $x^2 - 5x + 6$, the other factor is

   (A) $x - 2$ (B) $x + 2$ (C) $x + 3$ (D) $x - 3$

6. The factors of $3x^2 + 2x - 5$ are

   (A) $(3x - 5)(x + 1)$
   (B) $(3x - 1)(x + 5)$
   (C) $(3x + 5)(x - 1)$
   (D) $(3x + 1)(x - 5)$

7. If $3x^2$ is a factor of $12x^4 - 3x^3 + 6x^2$, the other factor is

   (A) $4x^2 - x + 2$ (B) $4x^2 - 3x^3 + 6x^2$
   (C) $4x^2 - 3x + 2$ (D) $4x^2 - x$

8. Factor $x^3 + x^2 - 12x$ completely.

   (A) $x(x + 4)(x - 3)$ (B) $(x^2 + 4x)(x - 3)$
   (C) $x(x + 6)(x - 2)$ (D) $x(x^2 + x + 12)$

9. Factor $2x^2 - 32$ completely.

   (A) $(2x + 8)(x - 4)$ (B) $2(x + 8)(x - 8)$
   (C) $(x + 4)(2x - 8)$ (D) $2(x + 4)(x - 4)$

10. The factors of $x^2 - 13x - 48$ are

    (A) $(x + 16)(x + 3)$
    (B) $(x - 8)(x - 6)$
    (C) $(x - 16)(x + 3)$
    (D) $(x + 4)(x - 12)$

11. Factor $2x^2 + 2$ completely.

    (A) $(2x + 1)(x + 1)$ (B) $(2x + 2)(x + 1)$
    (C) $2(x + 1)(x + 1)$ (D) $2(x^2 + 1)$

12. Factor $m^3n^4 + 2m^2n^2 - 4mn^3$.

(A) $mn^2(m^2n^2 + 2m - 4n)$

(B) $mn^2(mn^2 + 2m - 4n)$

(C) $m^2n^2(mn^2 + 2m - 4n)$

(D) $m^3n^3(n + 2 - 4m)$

13. Factor $\frac{16}{25}m^2 - 16n^2$.

(A) $\left(\frac{4}{5}m - 8n\right)\left(\frac{4}{5}m + 8n\right)$

(B) $\left(\frac{4}{5}m - 4n\right)\left(\frac{4}{5}m + 4n\right)$

(C) $\left(\frac{4}{5}m - 4n\right)\left(\frac{4}{5}m - 4n\right)$

(D) $\left(\frac{8}{5}m + 4n\right)\left(\frac{8}{5}m - 4n\right)$

14. The factors of $6z^2 + 7z - 20$ are

(A) $(6z - 5)(z + 4)$

(B) $(3z - 2)(2z + 10)$

(C) $(3z + 4)(2z - 5)$

(D) $(3z - 4)(2z + 5)$

15. If the expression $25K^3 - 15K^2 + 5K$ has a factor $5K$, then the other factor is

(A) $5K^2 - 3K$

(B) $5K^2 - 3K + 1$

(C) $5K^2 - 3K + K$

(D) $3K^2$

16. Factor $a^4 - b^4$ completely.

(A) $(a + b)^2(a - b)^2$

(B) $(a^2 + b^2)(a^2 - b^2)$

(C) $(a^2 + b^2)(a - b)(a + b)$

(D) $(a^2 + b^2)^2$

17. The expression $\left(\frac{y^2 - 9}{y^2 - 3y - 18}\right)\left(\frac{y - 6}{2y - 6}\right)$ is equivalent to

(A) 0

(B) $\frac{y - 6}{2(y + 6)}$

(C) $\frac{1}{2}$

(D) 1

18. The expression $\frac{x^2 - 16}{2} \div \frac{2x - 8}{6}$ is equivalent to

(A) $\frac{3}{2}(x + 4)$

(B) $\frac{(x + 4)(x - 4)^2}{6}$

(C) $\frac{3}{2}(x - 4)$

(D) $\frac{2}{3(x + 4)}$

19. Express as a fraction in *lowest terms*: $\frac{y^2 - 9}{2y + 6} \div \frac{y - 3}{y + 2}$.

(A) $\frac{(y - 3)^2}{2(y + 2)}$

(B) $\frac{y + 2}{2}$

(C) $y + 2$

(D) $y + 1$

20. The fraction $\frac{2x - 10}{x^2 - 25}$ is equivalent to

(A) $\frac{2x - 2}{x^2 - 5}$

(B) $\frac{2}{x - 5}$

(C) 0

(D) $\frac{2}{x + 5}$

EQUATIONS

1. If $4x + 3 = 2x + 4$, then $x =$

   (A) $-\frac{1}{2}$ (B) $\frac{1}{2}$ (C) 1   (D) $\frac{1}{6}$

2. If $5(y - 2) = 3y + 4$, then $y =$

   (A) 1   (B) $1\frac{3}{4}$ (C) 3   (D) 7

3. If $dy - c = a$, the value of y in terms of a and d is

   (A) $\frac{ac}{d}$ (B) $a + \frac{c}{d}$ (C) $\frac{a + c}{d}$ (D) $\frac{d}{a + c}$

4. Solve the equation $x^2 - 5x + 6 = 0$.

   (A) 1, 6   (B) 3, 2   (C) $-6, 1$ (D) $3, -2$

5. If $y = 3$ and $x = y - 3$, then $x =$

   (A) -6 (B) 0   (C) 6   (D) -9

6. If $y = 3x + 1$ and $x = y - 3$, then $y =$

   (A) -4 (B) -1 (C) 1   (D) 4

7. If $3z = 2(5 - z)$, then $z =$

   (A) 2   (B) $2\frac{1}{2}$ (C) 5   (D) 10

8. The positive root of $2x^2 = 72$ is

   (A) -6 (B) 6   (C) 18   (D) 1296

9. If $y = 2x$ and $x + y = 6$, then $x =$

   (A) 0   (B) 2   (C) 3   (D) 4

10. If $a + bx = c$, the value of x in terms of a, b, and c is

    (A) $\frac{c}{b} - a$ (B) $\frac{ac}{b}$ (C) $\frac{c - a}{b}$ (D) $c - \frac{a}{b}$

11. If $2x - y = 7$, then $y =$

(A) $2x + 7$ (B) $-2x + 7$
(C) $-5x$ (D) $2x - 7$

12. If $\frac{5}{y} + 3y = \frac{17}{y}$, then $y =$

(A) -2 and 2 (B) -2
(C) 2 (D) -3 and 3

13. If $0.03c = 6$, then $c =$

(A) 2 (B) 20 (C) 200 (D) 2000

14. If $4x - 3y = 15$ and $3y = 9 - 2x$, then $x =$

(A) 1 (B) 3 (C) 4 (D) 12

15. If $9y + 10 - x = 12$ and $x = 5y$, then $y =$

(A) $\frac{1}{7}$ (B) $\frac{1}{2}$ (C) $1\frac{4}{7}$ (D) $5\frac{1}{2}$

16. All of the following pairs of numbers are solutions of the equation $3x - 2y = 4$ EXCEPT

(A) $(3, 2\frac{1}{2})$ (B) $(-2, -5)$ (C) $(4, 4)$ (D) $(-2, 0)$

17. A point on the graph of $x + 3y = 13$ is

(A) $(4, -3)$ (B) $(4, 4)$ (C) $(-5, 6)$ (D) $(-2, 3)$

18. If the graph of the equation $2x + 5y = 4$ passes through the point with coordinates $(7, a)$, the value of a is

(A) $-15\frac{1}{2}$ (B) -2 (C) $3\frac{3}{5}$ (D) $19\frac{1}{2}$

19. If $\frac{2t}{5} - 4 = \frac{2t}{3}$, then $t =$

(A) -15 (B) $-3\frac{3}{4}$ (C) -1 (D) 15

20. The point $(2, -1)$ lies on the graph of ALL of the following EXCEPT

(A) $3x + y = 5$ (B) $2x + y = 3$
(C) $4x - y = 6$ (D) $2x - y = 5$

RATIO AND PROPORTION

1. If $\frac{x+1}{8} = \frac{9}{24}$, then $x =$

   (A) 2   (B) $2\frac{23}{24}$ (C) $20\frac{1}{3}$

   (D) It cannot be determined from the information given.

2. If 20 percent of a number is 18, what is the number?

   (A) 3.6   (B) 9   (C) 90   (D) 900

3. If x apples cost 25 cents, the number of apples which can be bought for 75 cents is

   (A) $\frac{x}{3}$ (B) $\frac{1875}{x}$ (C) $3x$

   (D) It cannot be determined from the information given.

4. If $\frac{1}{2}$ inch represents 3 feet in a scale drawing, then the number of inches that represents 24 feet is

   (A) $\frac{1}{16}$ (B) 4   (C) 16

   (D) It cannot be determined from the information given.

5. A girl 5 feet tall is standing near a tree 30 feet high. If the girl's shadow is 4 feet long, the length of the shadow of the tree is

   (A) $\frac{2}{3}$ feet   (B) 24 feet   (C) $37\frac{1}{2}$ feet

   (D) It cannot be determined from the information given.

6. Two numbers are in the ratio $1:5$ and their sum is 54. The smaller number is

   (A) 8   (B) 9   (C) 10   (D) 45

7. The number of feet in a inches is

   (A) $\frac{a}{12}$ (B) $\frac{12}{a}$ (C) $12a$ (D) $36a$

8. A grocer sold a pounds of butter for b cents. The number of cents the grocer received for x pounds of butter, expressed in terms of a and b, was

   (A) $\frac{ax}{b}$ (B) $\frac{a}{bx}$ (C) $\frac{b}{ax}$ (D) $\frac{bx}{a}$

9. On a map, if one inch represents 60 miles, then the number of miles represented by $2\frac{1}{2}$ inches is

   (A) $\frac{1}{24}$ (B) 24   (C) 150

   (D) It cannot be determined from the information given

10. If $\frac{y}{9} = \frac{y+1}{12}$, then $y =$

    (A) $\frac{1}{21}$ (B) $\frac{1}{3}$ (C) $\frac{3}{7}$ (D) 3

11. If 20% of a number is 8, then the number is

(A) 1.6   (B) 40   (C) 250
(D) It cannot be determined from the information given.

12. Marie earns $(d + 5)$ dollars per hour. If she worked h hours, the amount of money she earned is

(A) $h(d + 5)$ (B) $\frac{h}{d + 5}$ (C) $\frac{d + 5}{h}$
(D) It cannot be determined from the information given.

13. A school basketball team won 25 of the 40 games it played. What percent of the games played did the team win?

(A) 25%   (B) $37\frac{1}{2}\%$ (C) 40%   (D) $62\frac{1}{2}\%$

14. A vertical flagpole casts a shadow 16 m long at the same time that a nearby tree 5 m in height casts a shadow 4 m long. The height of the flagpole is

(A) $12\frac{4}{5}$ m   (B) $1\frac{1}{4}$ m   (C) 20 m
(D) It cannot be determined from the information given.

15. The number of inches in $(3x - 2)$ feet is

(A) $36x - 24$ (B) $36x - 2$
(C) $\frac{12}{3x - 2}$ (D) $\frac{3x - 2}{12}$

16. Calvin bought 16 tickets to a school swimming meet. This number was 25% of all the tickets sold by students. The number of tickets sold by students was

(A) 4   (B) 64   (C) $156\frac{1}{4}$
(D) It cannot be determined from the information given.

17. If 30 students took an examination and 24 passed, the percent of students who passed the examination is

(A) 20%   (B) 25%   (C) 75%   (D) 80%

18. If $\frac{x + 5}{8} = \frac{x - 1}{4}$, then $x =$

(A) $1\frac{1}{2}$ (B) $3\frac{1}{4}$ (C) $5\frac{1}{4}$ (D) 7

19. If $\frac{5}{x} = \frac{x}{20}$, then $x =$

(A) 10   (B) -10
(C) $+10$ and -10 (D) $+50$ and -50

20. If $xy = wz$, then

(A) $\frac{x}{z} = \frac{w}{y}$ (B) $\frac{x}{z} = \frac{y}{w}$ (C) $\frac{x}{y} = \frac{w}{z}$ (D) $\frac{x}{y} = \frac{z}{w}$

PROBABILITY

1. Two coins are tossed, a penny and a dime. The number of possible outcomes is

   (A) 1   (B) 2   (C) 3   (D) 4

2. How many different two-digit numbers can be formed using each of the digits 3, 5, and 7 only once?

   (A) 3   (B) 6   (C) 9   (D) 12

3. A box contains four slips of paper, each with one of the letters *g*, *a*, *t*, or *e* written on it. The number of three-letter outcomes that may be selected is

   (A) 12   (B) 24   (C) 36   (D) 48

4. From 6 students, 4 boys and 2 girls, a teacher wishes to pick a boy and a girl. The number of possible outcomes is

   (A) 4   (B) 7   (C) 8   (D) 15

5. Two dice are tossed. The number of ways 8 can appear as the sum is

   (A) 0   (B) 4   (C) 5   (D) 6

6. If the probability of an event's happening is $\frac{3}{7}$, the probability of the event's not happening is

   (A) $\frac{3}{4}$ (B) $\frac{4}{7}$ (C) $\frac{4}{3}$ (D) $\frac{3}{7}$

7. Two dice are tossed. The probability of obtaining a sum of 12 is

   (A) $\frac{1}{36}$ (B) $\frac{1}{6}$ (C) $\frac{1}{18}$ (D) $\frac{35}{36}$

8. Two coins are tossed. The probability of tossing one head and one tail is

   (A) $\frac{1}{4}$ (B) $\frac{1}{2}$ (C) $\frac{3}{4}$ (D) 1

9. If a girl has 5 blouses and 3 pair of slacks, the number of possible outfits consisting of one blouse and one pair of slacks is

   (A) 2   (B) 8   (C) 15   (D) $\frac{3}{5}$

10. The number of different ways 5 students can be arranged in a row is

    (A) 5   (B) 15   (C) 25   (D) 120

11. A card is drawn from an ordinary deck of 52 playing cards. The probability of drawing a heart is

    (A) $\frac{1}{52}$ (B) $\frac{1}{4}$ (C) $\frac{3}{4}$ (D) $\frac{51}{52}$

12. There are 3 red, 2 green, and 5 yellow buttons in a bag. The buttons are thoroughly mixed and one is drawn at random from the bag. The probability of drawing a red button is

(A) $\frac{1}{5}$ (B) $\frac{3}{10}$ (C) $\frac{1}{2}$ (D) 1

13. Mr. Sweeney bought 12 chances on a car that is to be raffled. If 6000 chances are sold, the probability that Mr. Sweeney will not win is

(A) 0   (B) $\frac{1}{500}$ (C) $\frac{499}{500}$ (D) 1

14. One letter of the name "Julane" is selected at random. The probability that the letter is a vowel is

(A) 0   (B) $\frac{1}{6}$ (C) $\frac{1}{3}$ (D) $\frac{1}{2}$

15. From a standard deck of 52 cards, one card is drawn. The probability that it will be either a jack, queen, or king is

(A) $\frac{3}{52}$ (B) $\frac{3}{13}$ (C) $\frac{10}{13}$ (D) 1

16. A jar contains 2 red marbles, 4 blue marbles, and 3 yellow marbles. If a single marble is picked at random from the jar, the probability that a red or a yellow marble is picked is

(A) $\frac{5}{9}$ (B) $\frac{2}{3}$ (C) $\frac{7}{9}$ (D) $\frac{2}{9}$

17. If the probability of Jones' *not* winning an election is 0.6, the probability that Jones will win the election is

(A) 0.3   (B) 0.4   (C) 0.5
(D) It cannot be determined from the information given.

18. The number of different arrangements of four digits that can be formed from the digits 2, 5, 6, and 8, if each digit is used only once in each arrangement, is

(A) 4   (B) 12   (C) 24   (D) 28

19. A box contains 4 dimes, 3 nickels, and 2 pennies. One coin is drawn, put aside, and then another coin is drawn. The probability that the two coins drawn total 9¢ is

(A) 0   (B) $\frac{1}{72}$ (C) $\frac{1}{6}$
(D) It cannot be determined from the information given.

20. A school cafeteria offers 6 kinds of sandwiches and 4 kinds of beverages. If a lunch consists of a sandwich and a fruit, how many different lunches can a student choose?

(A) 2   (B) 10   (C) 24
(D) It cannot be determined from the information given.

INEQUALITIES

1. If $a < 0$, then

   (A) $a + 1 > 0$ (B) $a - 3 < 0$

   (C) $a^2 < a$ (D) $2a > 0$

2. If $x > y$ and $y > z$, then

   (A) $xy > yz$ (B) $xyx > 0$

   (C) $x + y > z$ (D) $x > z$

3. If $2 + 3x > x - 4$, then

   (A) $x > -3$ (B) $x > -1$

   (C) $x > -\frac{3}{2}$ (D) $x > -\frac{1}{2}$

4. If $a > b$, then

   (A) $a - b < 0$ (B) $a^2 > b^2$

   (C) $ab > 0$ (D) $3a > 3b$

5. If x is an integer and if $-6 < x \le -2$, then x must be

   (A) $-6, -5, -4, -3, -2$ (B) $-6, -5, -4, -3$

   (C) $-5, -4, -3, -2$

   (D) It cannot be determined from the information given.

6. An expression equivalent to $1 < 3x - 4$ is

   (A) $x > \frac{5}{3}$ (B) $x < \frac{5}{3}$ (C) $x > -1$ (D) $x < -1$

7. If $x + 3y < 7$ and $(1, k)$ is an element of the solution set, then k could be equal to

   (A) 2   (B) 4   (C) 1   (D) 5

8. If $2 - 3x < x + 2$, then

   (A) $x < 0$ (B) $x > 0$ (C) $x > 1$ (D) $x < 1$

9.

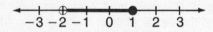

The inequality represented by this graph is

   (A) $-2 \le x \le 1$ (B) $-2 \le x < 1$

   (C) $-2 < x < 1$ (D) $-2 < x \le 1$

10. The largest possible value of y in the solution set of $3y + 1 \le 10$ is

   (A) 3   (B) -4 (C) 4   (D) 2

11. Which of the following is the graph of all x values such that $-3 \le x < 2$?

(A)

(B)

(C)

(D)

12. If $8x \ge 3(x - 5)$, then

(A) $x > -3$ (B) $x > -1$ (C) $x \ge -3$ (D) $x \ge -1$

13. If $y > -2x + 7$ and $(2, k)$ is an element of the solution set, then k could equal

(A) -1 (B) 3 (C) 0 (D) 5

14. The inequality $3(3x + 2) > 2(x + 8)$ is equivalent to

(A) $x > \frac{2}{7}$ (B) $x > \frac{6}{7}$ (C) $x > 1\frac{3}{7}$ (D) $x > 2$

15. If $x^2 + 4x < 0$, then which of the following is impossible?

(A) $x > 0$ (B) $x > -4$ (C) $x < 0$ (D) $x < -1$

16. If x is an integer and $-1 < 2x - 5 \le 3$, then x must be

(A) $2, 3, 4$ (B) 3 (C) 4 (D) $3, 4$

17. If $-4x > -8$, then

(A) $x < -2$ (B) $x > -2$ (C) $x > 2$ (D) $x < 2$

18. If $a > b$ and $a > c$, then

(A) $b < c$ (B) $2a > b + c$
(C) $b - a > c$ (D) $b + c > a$

19. If $a, x, y,$ and z are positive integers and $a < x, z > x$, and $y > z$, then

(A) $y < a$ (B) $2a > x + y$
(C) $y - a > x - a$ (D) $x > y$

20.
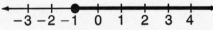

The inequality represented by the graph is

(A) $x \ge -1$ (B) $x > -1$
(C) $x < -1$ (D) $x \le -1$

PROBLEM SOLVING

1. Two angles of a triangle are equal in measure and the measure of the third angle is 130°. The number of degrees in one of the two equal angles is

   (A) 15 (B) 25 (C) 50 (D) 75

2. Two positive numbers are consecutive odd integers. The square of the smaller is 4 more than 3 times the larger. The smaller integer is

   (A) 3 (B) 5 (C) 7 (D) 9

3. The length of a rectangle is 8 meters more than its width. If the perimeter is 56 meters, the length of the rectangle is

   (A) 10 m (B) 18 m (C) 24 m (D) $3\frac{1}{9}$ m

4. The longer leg of a right triangle is 7 more than the shorter leg. The hypotenuse is 9 more than the shorter leg. If the perimeter of the triangle is 40, the length of the hypotenuse is

   (A) 8 (B) 15 (C) 17 (D) 18

5. Tickets for a dance cost $.75 each if purchased in advance, but are $1 each if purchased at the door. If 100 tickets were sold and $85 was collected, how many tickets were sold at the door?

   (A) 40 (B) 60 (C) 65 (D) 70

6. A two-digit number is 6 times the sum of its digits. Two times the units digit is three more than the tens digit. The units digit is

   (A) 2 (B) 3 (C) 4 (D) 5

7. A mechanic's hourly wage is three times her helper's. They were paid a total of $68 for a job on which the mechanic worked 4 hours and the helper worked 5 hours. The hourly wage of the mechanic is

   (A) $4 (B) $12 (C) $17 (D) $51

8. Part of $7200 was invested at 6% and the rest was invested at 7%. The total annual income from these investments is $464. The number of dollars invested at 6% is

   (A) 800 (B) 3200 (C) 4000 (D) 6400

9. Bill paid $16.35 for 80 postage stamps. If some were 22¢ stamps and the rest were 17¢ stamps, the number of 22¢ stamps is

   (A) 7 (B) 13 (C) 25 (D) 55

10. Two women start from the same place at the same time. One travels due west at a rate of 50 mph and the other travels due east at a rate of 55 mph. In how many hours will they be 420 miles apart?

    (A) 3 (B) 4 (C) 5 (D) 6

11. Sam takes twice as long as Tom to paint a certain wall. Together they can paint the wall in 6 hours. How long would it take Sam to paint the wall alone.?

(A) $\frac{1}{2}$ hour (B) 4 hours (C) 9 hours (D) 18 hours

12. Grace wants an equal number of pennies, nickels, and dimes for her savings of $2.40. How many of each kind of coin will she have?

(A) 15 (B) 20 (C) 25 (D) 30

13. Jane is 6 years older than Jim. Six years ago she was twice as old as he was. How old is Jane now?

(A) 6 (B) 10 (C) 12 (D) 18

14. The first angle of a triangle is twice the second and the third is 20 degrees larger than the second angle. Find the number of degrees in the measure of the smallest angle of the triangle.

(A) 40 (B) 50 (C) 60 (D) 80

15. One positive number is 2 more than another. The sum of their squares is 34. The smaller number is

(A) −5 (B) −3 (C) 3 (D) 5

16. The smallest of three consecutive integers whose sum is less than 86 is

(A) 27 (B) 28 (C) 29 (D) 30

17. I have 20 coins consisting of nickels and quarters. If the value of the coins is $4.40, how many are nickels?

(A) 3 (B) 15 (C) 5 (D) 17

18. The length of a rectangle is 1cm less than twice its width. If the perimeter of the rectangle is 76cm, the number of centimeters in the width of the rectangle is

(A) 13 (B) 25 (C) 26 (D) 51

19. Mae bicycled from her home to school at 8 mph. She returned home at 4 mph. If the round trip took 3 hours, how many miles is it from school to Mae's home?

(A) 1 (B) 2 (C) 4 (D) 8

20. 850 people attended the school play. The tickets for students were $1.50 each, and adult tickets were $2 each. If the total receipts were $1650, how many adult tickets were sold?

(A) 100 (B) 150 (C) 700 (D) 750

Answer Key to Practice Tests

Following each answer, there is a number or numbers in the form "*a.b*" in parentheses. This number refers to the Refresher Section (beginning on page 23). The number "*a*" indicates the Math area of the problem:

1. Integers
2. Algebraic Expressions
3. Factoring
4. Equations

5. Ratio and Proportion
6. Probability
7. Inequalities
8. Problem Solving

The number "*b*" indicates the section in the Math area that explains the rule or method used in solving the problem.

INTEGERS

1. C (1.2, 1.1)
2. B (1.5, 1.4)
3. C (1.7, 4.2, 2.1)
4. A (1.4)
5. C (1.6)
6. A (1.6, 2.1, 1.2)
7. A (1.2, 2.6)
8. C (1.3, 1.5)
9. D (1.4, 1.6, 1.8)
10. C (1.5)

11. A (1.4)
12. B (1.8, 1.7)
13. A (1.8)
14. D (1.4, 1.5)
15. C (1.2, 1.1)
16. D (1.4, 1.8, 1.3)
17. D (1.8)
18. A (1.5, 2.6)
19. A (1.1)
20. C (1.7, 1.6)

ALGEBRAIC EXPRESSIONS

1. B (2.7, 2.8)
2. A (2.9)
3. A (2.6, 2.1)
4. B (2.7, 1.5, 2.8)
5. C (2.8, 2.7)
6. C (2.9)
7. B (2.10)
8. C (2.3, 2.8)
9. A (2.10, 2.9)
10. D (2.7, 2.8)

11. C (2.1)
12. D (2.10)
13. B (2.3)
14. D (2.1)
15. A (2.9)
16. D (2.6, 2.1)
17. C (2.11, 2.1)
18. B (2.7, 2.8)
19. B (2.11)
20. D (2.11)

FACTORING

1. C (3.3)
2. D (3.4, 2.9)
3. B (3.2)
4. B (3.3)
5. A (3.5, 2.9)
6. C (3.5, 2.9)
7. A (3.3, 2.10)
8. A (3.6, 3.3, 3.5)
9. D (3.6, 3.3, 3.4)
10. C (3.5)
11. D (3.6, 3.3)
12. A (3.3)
13. B (3.4)
14. D (3.5, 2.9)
15. B (3.3)
16. C (3.6, 3.4)
17. C (3.5, 3.4, 3.3)
18. A (3.4, 3.3)
19. B (3.4, 3.3)
20. D (3.4, 3.3)

EQUATIONS

1. B (4.3, 4.2)
2. D (4.3, 4.2, 1.7)
3. C (4.5, 4.3)
4. B (4.4, 3.5)
5. B (4.6, 4.2)
6. D (4.6, 4.2)
7. A (4.3, 1.7)
8. B (4.4, 3.4)
9. B (4.2, 4.3)
10. C (4.3)
11. D (4.5, 4.3)
12. A (4.3, 4.4)
13. C (4.3)
14. C (4.5, 4.3)
15. B (4.5, 4.3)
16. D (4.3, 4.2)
17. C (4.10, 4.3)
18. B (4.10, 4.3)
19. A (4.3)
20. C (4.10, 4.3)

RATIO AND PROPORTION

1. A (5.4, 5.3)
2. C (5.5, 5.4)
3. C (5.5, 5.4)
4. B (5.5, 5.4, 5.1)
5. B (5.5, 5.4)
6. B (5.1, 2.3)
7. A (5.1, 5.4)
8. D (5.5, 5.4, 4.5)
9. C (5.5, 5.4)
10. D (5.4, 4.3)
11. B (5.5, 5.4)
12. A (5.5, 5.3, 5.4)
13. D (5.5, 5.4)
14. C (5.5, 5.4)
15. A (5.5, 5.4)
16. B (5.5, 5.4)
17. D (5.5, 5.4)
18. D (5.4, 4.3)
19. C (5.4, 4.4, 3.4)
20. A (5.3, 5.4)

PROBABILITY	**1.** D (6.1)	**11.** B (6.2)
	2. B (6.1)	**12.** B (6.2)
	3. B (6.1)	**13.** C (6.2)
	4. C (6.1)	**14.** D (6.2)
	5. C (6.1)	**15.** B (6.2)
	6. B (6.2)	**16.** A (6.2)
	7. A (6.2, 6.1)	**17.** B (6.2)
	8. B (6.2, 6.1)	**18.** C (6.1)
	9. C (6.1)	**19.** A (6.2, 6.1)
	10. D (6.1)	**20.** D (6.1)

INEQUALITIES	**1.** B (7.3)	**11.** B (7.6, 7.5)
	2. D (7.2, 7.3)	**12.** C (7.4, 7.3)
	3. A (7.3)	**13.** D (7.4, 7.3, 4.5)
	4. D (7.3)	**14.** C (7.4, 1.7)
	5. C (7.6, 7.5)	**15.** A (7.3)
	6. A (7.4, 7.3)	**16.** D (7.6, 7.4)
	7. C (7.4, 7.3, 4.5)	**17.** D (7.4, 7.3)
	8. B (7.4, 7.3)	**18.** B (7.3)
	9. D (7.6, 7.5)	**19.** C (7.2, 7.3)
	10. A (7.4, 7.1)	**20.** A (7.5)

PROBLEM SOLVING	**1.** B (8.10, 2.3, 4.3)	**11.** D (8.8, 2.3, 4.3)
	2. B (8.2, 2.3, 4.4)	**12.** A (8.5, 2.3, 4.3)
	3. B (8.10, 2.3, 4.3)	**13.** D (8.6, 2.3, 4.3)
	4. C (8.10, 2.3, 4.3)	**14.** A (8.10, 2.3, 4.3)
	5. A (8.7, 2.3, 4.3)	**15.** C (8.1, 2.3, 4.4)
	6. C (8.9, 2.3, 4.6)	**16.** A (8.2, 2.3, 7.4)
	7. B (8.7, 2.3, 4.3)	**17.** A (8.5, 2.3, 4.3)
	8. C (8.7, 2.3, 4.3)	**18.** A (8.10, 2.3, 4.3)
	9. D (8.5, 2.3, 4.3)	**19.** D (8.3, 2.3, 4.3)
	10. B (8.3, 2.3, 4.3)	**20.** D (8.7, 2.3, 4.3)

Solutions for Algebra Practice Tests

INTEGERS

1. (C) The expression $x + y$ will be a negative number only if $y < -x$.

> *If your choice was*
> (A), the condition $x = y$ leads to a positive, zero, or negative sum.
> (B), the condition $y > x$ leads to either a positive or a negative sum.
> (D), the condition $x < 0$ leads to either a positive or a negative sum.

2. (B) When a positive number is subtracted from a smaller positive number, the result is negative. $1 - 3 = -2$

> *If your choice was*
> (A), you added -1 and -3 and got -4.
> (C), you subtracted -3 from 1 and got $+4$.
> (D), you subtracted 1 from 3 and got $+2$.

3. (C) If $\frac{x}{y} = 1$, then x is equal to y. If $x = y = 2$, then $(x + y)^2 = z$ is $(2 + 2)^2 = z$, or $4^2 = z$, or $z = 16$.

> *If your choice was*
> (A), the number 5 cannot be the square of two integers.
> (B), then $x + y = 3$ and $x \neq y$.
> (D), then $x + y = 5$ and $x \neq y$.

4. (A) The sum of 3, -4, and y is $-1 + y$. This is the sum of y and -1.

> *If your choice was*
> (B), you found a sum of -7 for 3 and -4.
> (C), you found a sum of $+7$ for 3 and -4.
> (D), you did not answer the question asked.

5. (C) The product of an odd number of negative factors is always negative, so $(-1)(-2)(-3) = -6$ and $(-6)(+4) = -24$.

> *If your choice was*
> (A), you found the correct sign of the product but added the absolute values.
> (B), you found the correct product but the wrong sign.
> (D), you found the product of -1 and -2 as $+3$.

6. (A) The least value of $\left(-\frac{1}{2}\right)^N$ will occur when $\left(-\frac{1}{2}\right)^N$ is negative and the denominator is the least number. Therefore, N must be the least *odd* number. Therefore, $\left(-\frac{1}{2}\right)^3 = -\frac{1}{8}$.

If your choice was
(B or D), the value of $\left(-\frac{1}{2}\right)^N$ will be a positive number.
(C), the value of $\left(-\frac{1}{2}\right)^5 = -\frac{1}{32}$, which is greater than $-\frac{1}{8}$.

7. (A) Evaluate the expression for x equal to any integer and $y > 0$.

Let $x = -6$	Let $x = 0$	Let $x = 6$
$y = 3$	$y = 3$	$y = 3$
$-6 - 3 < -6 + 3$	$0 - 3 < 0 + 3$	$6 - 3 < 6 + 3$
$-9 < -3$	$-3 < 3$	$3 < 9$
True	True	True

If your choice was
(B), try $x = 6$ and $y = -3$. Then $6 - (-3) \overset{?}{<} 6 - 3$
$$6 + 3 \overset{?}{<} 3$$
$$9 \not< 3$$
(C), try $x = -2$ and $y = -2$. Then $-2 - (-2) \overset{?}{<} -2 + (-2)$
$$-2 + 2 \overset{?}{<} -4$$
$$0 \not< -4$$
(D), see (B) above.

8. (C) The value of $|-5| = 5$ and the value of $|2| = 2$. Thus, $|-5| - |2| = 5 - 2 = 3$.

If your choice was
(A), you evaluated $|-5|$ as -5.
(B), you evaluated $|-5|$ as -5 and incorrectly found the difference, $-5 - 2$, as -3.
(D), you found the sum of 5 and 2 instead of the difference.

9. (D) I. True. The sum of two positive numbers is always positive.
II. True. The product of two negative numbers is always positive.
III. True. The quotient of two positive numbers is always positive.

If your choice was
(A, B, or C), see the solution above.

10. (C) Change the sign of -5 and then add: $-2 + 5 = +3$.

If your choice was
(A), you added -2 and -5.
(B), you changed the sign of the minuend, -2, to $+2$ and added -5 and $+2$.
(D), you changed both -2 and -5 to $+2$ and $+5$ and then added.

11. (A) Add the absolute values of -5 and -2 and keep the common sign. Thus, $5 + 2 = 7$ and the common sign is negative. So, $(-5) + (-2) = -7$.

If your choice was
(B), you subtracted the absolute values.
(C), you subtracted the absolute values but did not keep the common sign.
(D), you failed to keep the common sign.

12. (B) The quotient of two negative numbers is always positive, so $(-15) \div (-3) = +5$. The sum of $+5$ and -5, two opposites, is always 0.

If your choice was
(A), you found the quotient of $(-15) \div (-3)$ as -5.
(C), you subtracted the absolute values instead of dividing.
(D), see (A) above, and then you multiplied instead of adding.

13. (A)
$$\left(\tfrac{1}{2}\right) \div \left(-\tfrac{7}{8}\right) = -\left(\tfrac{1}{2} \div \tfrac{7}{8}\right)$$
$$= -\left(\tfrac{1}{\cancel{2}} \times \tfrac{\cancel{8}^{4}}{7}\right) = -\tfrac{4}{7}$$

If your choice was
(B), you did not find the reciprocal of the divisor before multiplying.
(C), you found the reciprocal of $\tfrac{1}{2}$ instead of $\tfrac{7}{8}$.
(D), you found the reciprocals of both $\tfrac{1}{2}$ and $\tfrac{7}{8}$.

14. (D) First evaluate the expression inside the brackets.
$$[(-8) + (-2)] = -10$$
Then, $7 - (-10) = 7 + 10 = 17$.

If your choice was
(A), you added -10 and 7 instead of subtracting.
(B), you found $7 - (-8)$ incorrectly as $+1$ and then added -2.
(C), you found $7 - (-8)$ as 15 and then added -2.

15. (C)

The number line shows that $-7 < -5 < -2 < +5$.

If your choice was
(A, B, or D), see the solution above.

16. (D) $(-18) + (-2) = -20$ and $(+7) + (-2) = +5$

Thus, $\left|\frac{-20}{+5}\right| = |-4| = 4.$

If your choice was
(A), you forgot to find the absolute value.
(B), you found $(+7) + (-2)$ as $+9$.
(C), you found $(-18) + (-2)$ as -16.

17. (D) $\frac{-3}{6} = \frac{-1}{2}.$ The negative sign can be placed in the denominator or in front of the fraction.

Thus, $\frac{-1}{2} = \frac{1}{-2} = -\frac{1}{2}.$

If your choice was
(A, B, or C), see the solution above.

18. (A) Evaluate the expression $r - s$ for different values of r and s to see which will make $r - s$ a negative number.

Let $r = -3$	Let $r = 0$	Let $r = 6$
$s = +5$	$s = +2$	$s = +8$
$-3 - (+5) =$	$0 - (+2) =$	$6 - (+8) =$
$-3 + (-5) = -8$	$0 + (-2) = -2$	$6 + (-8) = -2$

Thus, a negative number appeared when $s > r$.

If your choice was
(B), evaluate $r - s$ when $s = 2$ and $r = 3$; $3 - 2 = +1$.
(C), see (B) above.
(D), since $r = s$, then $r - s = 0$.

19. (A) If you choose $n = 4$, then you are looking for an integer greater than $4 - 1$, or 3, and less than 4.

Thus, there are no integers between 3 and 4.

If your choice was
(B, C, or D), see the solution above.

20. (C) If $m \times n = p$ and $p \neq 0$, then $m \times n \neq 0$. For this to be true, neither m nor n can equal 0.

If your choice was
(A), use the relationship $3 \times 4 = 12$. Thus, $12 \div 3 = 4$.
(B), by the commutative property of multiplication, $m \times n = n \times m$.
(D), use the relationship $3 \times 4 = 12$. Thus, $12 \div 4 = 3$.

ALGEBRAIC EXPRESSIONS

1. (B) Terms can only be combined if they are like terms. The like terms are $2y^3$ and $3y^3$. So, $5x^3 + (2y^3 + 3y^3) = 5x^3 + 5y^3$.

If your choice was
(A), you added both the like and the unlike terms together.
(C), you added the exponents in the like terms.
(D), see (A) and (C) above.

2. (A)
$$(x + 1)(3x + 1) = (x + 1)\,3x + (x + 1)\,1$$
$$= 3x^2 + 3x + x + 1$$
$$= 3x^2 + 4x + 1$$

If your choice was
(B), you incorrectly added $3x$ and x as $3x$.
(C), you incorrectly multiplied 1 and 1 as 2.
(D), you incorrectly multiplied $3x$ and x as $4x^2$.

3. (A) Evaluate the expression for $a = 1$ and $b = 2$.
$$3a^3b^2 = 3(1)^3(2)^2$$
$$= 3(1)(4)$$
$$= 12$$

If your choice was
(B), you evaluated 1^3 as 3.
(C), you evaluated $3a^3$ as $(3 \cdot 1)^3$ or 27.
(D), see (C) above. Then $27(2)^2$ was evaluated
as 54^2 or 2916.

4. (B)
$$5x^2 - 2x + 3 - (3x^2 + 4x - 3) =$$
$$5x^2 - 2x + 3 - 3x^2 - 4x + 3 =$$
$$(5x^2 - 3x^2) + (-2x - 4x) + (+3 + 3) =$$
$$2x^2 \quad - \quad 6x \quad + \quad 6$$

If your choice was
(A), you did not change the signs of the terms in the
subtrahend.
(C), you subtracted $5x^2 - 2x + 3$ from $3x^2 + 4x - 3$.
(D), you changed only the sign of $3x^2$ when you subtracted.

5. (C) Since the denominators are the same, keep the denominator
and subtract the numerators. $\dfrac{9}{y} - \dfrac{3}{y} = \dfrac{6}{y}$

If your choice was
(A), you omitted the denominator.
(B), you wrote the denominator as part of the numerator.
(D), you subtracted the absolute values but chose the sign of
the number with the least absolute value.

6. (C) Multiply the numbers and letters separately.
First, $5 \cdot 4 = 20$ and then $z^2 \cdot z^3 = z^5$.
Thus, $(5z^2)(4z^3) = 20z^5$.

If your choice was
(A), you added the coefficients and multiplied the exponents.
(B), you multiplied the exponents.
(D), you added the coefficients.

7. (B) Divide the numbers and letters separately.

$$\frac{8x^4x^3}{2xy^3} = \frac{8}{2} \cdot \frac{x^4}{x} \cdot \frac{y^3}{y^3}$$

$$= 4 \cdot x^3 \cdot 1 = 4x^3$$

If your choice was
(A), you subtracted 2 from 8.
(C), you considered x as x^0 when you divided x^4 by x.
    x is equivalent to x^1.
(D), you left the base x out of the quotient.

8. (C) Since even integers increase by 2, the next larger even integer after $n - 2$ is $n - 2 + 2$, or n.

If your choice was
(A), you found the next smaller even integer.
(B), you found the next larger integer.
(D), you found the second larger even integer.

9. (A)

$$\begin{array}{r} 4n - 3 \\ n - 1\overline{)4n^2 - 7n + 3} \\ \underline{4n^2 - 4n} \\ -3n + 3 \\ -3n + 3 \end{array}$$

If your choice was
(B), you found the sum.
(C), you found the product.
(D), you subtracted $(-7n) - (-4n)$ incorrectly as $-11n$.

10. (D) 6 is the least common denominator.

$$\frac{x + 1}{2} = \frac{3(x + 1)}{6} \text{ and } \frac{x}{3} = \frac{2x}{6}$$

$$\frac{x + 1}{2} = \frac{3x + 3}{6}$$

Thus,

$$\frac{x+1}{2} + \frac{x}{3} = \frac{3x+3}{6} + \frac{2x}{6}$$

$$= \frac{3x+3+2x}{6}$$

$$= \frac{5x+3}{6}$$

If your choice was
(A), you added the numerators and the denominators.
(B), you multiplied 3 times $x + 1$ as $3x + 1$ when changing $\frac{x + 1}{2}$ to sixths.
(C), you combined like and unlike terms in the numerator.

11. (C) $\sqrt[3]{27} = 3$ since $3^3 = 27$.

$\sqrt[5]{32} = 2$ since $2^5 = 32$.

Thus, $\sqrt[3]{27} + \sqrt[5]{32} = 3 + 2 = 5$.

If your choice was
(A), you added the roots and added the numbers.
(B), you subtracted $3 - 2 = 1$.
(D), you multiplied $3 \cdot 2 = 6$.

12. (D)
$$\frac{12x^4 - 3x^3 + 6x^2}{3x^2} = \frac{12x^4}{3x^2} - \frac{3x^3}{3x^2} + \frac{6x^2}{3x^2}$$
$$= 4x^2 - x + 2$$

If your choice was
(A), you combined the terms in the numerator:
$12x^4 - 3x^3 + 6x^2 \neq 15x^4$.
(B), you did not divide the coefficient in the first term.
(C), you did not divide the coefficient in the second term.

13. (B) n multiplied by 3 is represented by $3n$. Nineteen less than this is $3n - 19$.

If your choice was
(A), you divided n by 3.
(C), you subtracted three times the number from 19.
(D), you incorrectly combined $3n$ and -19.

14 (D)
$$(2x^3)^3 = (2x^3)(2x^3)(2x^3)$$
$$= (2 \cdot 2 \cdot 2)(x^3 \cdot x^3 \cdot x^3)$$
$$= 8x^9$$

If your choice was
(A), you added $2 + 2 + 2 = 6$.
(B), you added $2 + 2 + 2 = 6$ and multiplied the exponents.
(C), you multiplied the exponents.

15. (A)
$$(a - b)(c + 2d) = (a - b)c + (a - b)(2d)$$
$$= ac - bc + 2ad - 2bd$$
$$= ac + 2ad - bc - 2bd$$

If your choice was
(B), you multiplied by $a + b$ instead of $a - b$.
(C), you added all the coefficients (3) and multiplied the letters.
(D), you multiplied only the two first terms and the two last terms.

16. (D)
$$(xy)^2 = (-3 \cdot 2)^2$$
$$= (-6)^2 = 36$$

If your choice was
(A), you incorrectly placed a negative sign in the answer.
(B), you added $-3 + 2 = (-1)^2 = 1$.
(C), you multiplied 6 by 2.

17. (C) Evaluate the expression for each of the given values.

(A) $-1 * -1 = \frac{1}{(-1)^2} + (-1)^2 = \frac{1}{1} + 1 = 2 \qquad 2 \neq 1$

(B) $1 * 1 = \frac{1}{1^2} + 1^2 = \frac{1}{1} + 1 = 2 \qquad 2 \neq 1$

(C) $1 * 0 = \frac{1}{1^2} + 0^2 = \frac{1}{1} + 0 = 1$

(D) $-1 * 1 = \frac{1}{(-1)^2} + 1^2 = \frac{1}{1} + 1 = 2 \qquad 2 \neq 1$

18. (B) The sum of $2 + 3x$ and $3x^2 - 3x + 4$ is $3x^2 + 6$.
Therefore,
$$3x^2 + 6 - (5 - 3x) =$$
$$3x^2 + 6 - 5 + 3x =$$
$$3x^2 + 3x + 1$$

If your choice was
(A), you added $+3x$ and $-3x$ incorrectly.
(C), you found the sum of $3x^2 + 6$ and $5 - 3x$.
(D), you subtracted $3x^2 + 6$ from $5 - 3x$.

19. (B) If $a \oplus b = \frac{b+1}{a}$, then

$$2 \oplus 3 = \frac{3+1}{2} = \frac{4}{2} = 2,$$

and $(2 \oplus 3) \oplus 1 = 2 \oplus 1$

$$2 \oplus 1 = \frac{1+1}{2} = \frac{2}{2} = 1$$

Thus, $(2 \oplus 3) \oplus 1 = 1$.

If your choice was
(A), you first found $(3 \oplus 1)$ and then $2 \oplus (3 \oplus 1)$.
(C), you substituted 2 for b and 3 for a.
(D), you found $2 \oplus 3$ correctly, but substituted 2 for b and 1 for a in $2 \oplus 1$.

20. (D) If $r * s = \frac{r+s}{2} - 1$

then, $1 * 1 = \frac{1+1}{2} - 1$

$= \frac{2}{2} - 1 = 1 - 1 = 0$

If your choice was

(A), $r * 0 = \frac{r+0}{2} - 1 = \frac{r}{2} - 1$

(B), $s * 0 = \frac{s+0}{2} - 1 = \frac{s}{2} - 1$

(C), $r * -r = \frac{r+(-r)}{2} - 1 = \frac{0}{2} - 1 = -1$

FACTORING

1. (C) A common factor is an expression that divides into all the terms of the given expression.

$$3x^2y + 6x = 3 \cdot x \cdot x \cdot y + 2 \cdot 3 \cdot x$$

The common factors are 3 and x. Thus, the greatest common factor of $3x^2y + 6x$ is $3x$.

If your choice was

(A), you found a common factor, but not the greatest common factor.

(B), see (A) above.

(D), y is not a factor of $6x$.

2. (D) The factors of the difference of two squares are the sum and the difference of the square roots.

Therefore, $x^2 - 49 = (x + 7)(x - 7)$.

If your choice was

(A), x is not a factor of 49.

(B), $(x - 7)(x - 7) = x^2 - 14x + 49$.

(C), $(x^2 - 7)(x^2 + 7) = x^4 - 49$.

3. (B) Use a factor tree to find the prime factorization.

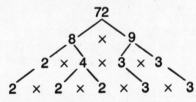

So, $72 = 2 \times 2 \times 2 \times 3 \times 3 = 2^3 \times 3^2$

If your choice was
(A), 72 is not a prime number.
(C), 4 is not a prime number.
(D), 12 is not a prime number.

4. **(B)** The common factor of $6a$ and 9 is 3.
Therefore, $6a - 9 = 3\left(\frac{6a}{3} - \frac{9}{3}\right) = 3(2a - 3)$.

If your choice was
(A), 2 is not a factor of 9.
(C), 6 is not a factor of 9.
(D), you did not find that 3 is a common factor of both
$6a$ and 9.

5. **(A)** $x^2 - 5x + 6$ is a trinomial. The factors of the first term are
both x. By trial and error, $x^2 - 5x + 6$ is factored into
$(x - 3)(x - 2)$. Thus, $x - 2$ is the other factor.

If your choice was
(B), the product of $(x - 3)(x + 2)$ is $x^2 - x - 6$.
(C), the product of $(x - 3)(x + 3)$ is $x^2 - 9$.
(D), the product of $(x - 3)(x - 3)$ is $x^2 - 6x + 9$.

6. **(C)** $3x^2 + 2x - 5$ is a trinomial of the form $ax^2 + bx + c$ where
$a \neq 1$. The factors of $3x^2$ are x and $3x$. The factors of -5 are
1 and -5, or -1 and 5. By trial and error, $3x^2 + 2x - 5$ is
factored into $(3x + 5)(x - 1)$.

If your choice was
(A), $(3x - 5)(x + 1) = 3x^2 - 2x - 5$.
(B), $(3x - 1)(x + 5) = 3x^2 + 14x - 5$.
(D), $(3x + 1)(x - 5) = 3x^2 - 14x - 5$.

7. **(A)** If $3x^2$ is a factor, then it divides each term of $12x^4 - 3x^3 + 6x^2$.

$$\frac{12x^4 - 3x^3 + 6x^2}{3x^2} = \frac{12x^4}{3x^2} - \frac{3x^3}{3x^2} + \frac{6x^2}{3x^2}$$
$$= 4x^2 - x + 2$$

If your choice was
(B), you failed to divide $-3x^3 + 6x^2$ by $3x^2$.
(C), you forgot to divide the coefficients of $-3x^3$ and $3x^2$.
(D), you forgot to include the quotient of $6x^2$ and $3x^2$ in
your answer.

8. (A) To factor $x^3 + x^2 - 12x$ completely, factor out the common factor x.
$$x^3 + x^2 - 12x = x(x^2 + x - 12)$$
Then factor the trinomial to get $x(x + 4)(x - 3)$.

If your choice was
(B), $x^2 + 4x$ is not completely factored since x is a common factor.
(C), $x(x + 6)(x - 2) = x^3 + 4x^2 - 12x$
(D), $x^2 + x - 12$ is a trinomial which can be factored.

9. (D) To factor $2x^2 - 32$ completely, factor out the common factor 2.
$$2x^2 - 32 = 2(x^2 - 16)$$

Then factor the difference of two squares to get
$$2(x + 4)(x - 4).$$

If your choice was
(A), $2x + 8$ has a common factor of 2.
(B), you factored 16 as 8×8 instead of 4×4.
(C), $2x - 8$ has a common factor of 2.

10. (C) $x^2 - 13x - 48$ is a trinomial. The factors of the first term are both x. By trial and error, $x^2 - 13x - 48$ is factored into $(x - 16)(x + 3)$.

If your choice was
(A), $(x + 16)(x + 3) = x^2 + 19x + 48$
(B), $(x - 8)(x - 6) = x^2 - 14x + 48$
(D), $(x + 4)(x - 12) = x^2 - 8x - 48$

11. (D) First factor out the common factor 2 to get $2(x^2 + 1)$.
Since $x^2 + 1$ is not the difference of two squares, the binomial is completely factored.

If your choice was
(A), $(2x + 1)(x + 1) = 2x^2 + 3x + 1$
(B), $(2x + 2)(x + 1) = 2x^2 + 4x + 2$
(C), $2(x + 1)(x + 1) = 2(x^2 + 2x + 1) = 2x^2 + 4x + 2$

12. (A) Factor out the greatest common factor mn^2.
$$\frac{m^3n^4}{mn^2} + \frac{2m^2n^2}{mn^2} - \frac{4mn^3}{mn^2} = m^2n^2 + 2m - 4n$$
Thus, $m^3n^4 + 2m^2n^2 - 4mn^3 = mn^2(m^2n^2 + 2m - 4n)$.

If your choice was
(B), you divided m^3n^4 by mn^2 incorrectly.
(C), you did not choose a common factor for each term of the expression.
(D), see (C) above.

13. **(B)** The factors of the difference of two squares are the sum and the difference of the square roots.

Therefore, $\frac{16}{25}m^2 - 16n^2 = \left(\frac{4}{5}m - 4n\right)\left(\frac{4}{5}m + 4n\right)$.

If your choice was
(A), the product of $8n$ and $8n$ is $64n^2$.
(C), the product of $-4n$ and $-4n$ is $+16n^2$.
(D), the product of $\frac{8}{5}m$ and $\frac{8}{5}m$ is $\frac{64}{25}m^2$.

14. **(D)** The factors of $6z^2$ are z and $6z$, or $2z$ and $3z$. The factors of 20 are ± 1 and ± 20, or ± 2 and ± 10, or ± 4 and ± 5. Write down all possible pairs of binomial factors and then, by trial and error, $6z^2 + 7z - 20$ is factored into $(3z - 4)(2z + 5)$.

If your choice was
(A), $(6z - 5)(z + 4) = 6z^2 + 19z - 20$
(B), $(3z - 2)(2z + 10) = 6z^2 + 26z - 20$
(C), $(3z + 4)(2z - 5) = 6z^2 - 7z - 20$

15. **(B)** Factor out the common factor $5K$.
$$\frac{25K^3}{5K} - \frac{15K^2}{5K} + \frac{5K}{5K} = 5K^2 - 3K + 1$$

If your choice was
(A), you found that $5K \div 5K = 0$, but $5K \div 5K = 1$.
(C), you divided only the coefficients in $5K \div 5K$.
(D), you incorrectly combined all the terms in the expression $15K^3 \div 5K = 3K^2$.

16. **(C)** $a^4 - b^4$ is the difference of two squares, so
$$a^4 - b^4 = (a^2 + b^2)(a^2 - b^2)$$

$a^2 - b^2$ is the difference of two squares, so
$$a^4 - b^4 = (a^2 + b^2)(a^2 - b^2)$$
$$= (a^2 + b^2)(a - b)(a + b)$$

If your choice was
(A), you incorrectly factored $a^2 + b^2$ into $(a + b)(a - b)$.
(B), you did not factor $a^2 - b^2$ further.
(D), $(a^2 - b^2)^2 = a^4 - 2a^2b^2 + b^4$

17. **(C)** Factor each term if you can.
$$\left(\frac{y^2 - 9}{y^2 - 3y - 18}\right)\left(\frac{y - 6}{2y - 6}\right)$$
$$\frac{(y + 3)(y - 3)}{(y - 6)(y + 3)} \cdot \frac{y - 6}{2(y - 3)}$$

Then divide out the common factors.

$$\frac{\cancel{(y + 3)}^1\cancel{(y - 3)}^1}{\cancel{(y - 6)}_1\cancel{(y + 3)}_1} \cdot \frac{\cancel{y - 6}^1}{2\cancel{(y - 3)}_1} = \frac{1}{2}$$

If your choice was
(A), you thought that since all the terms in the numerator were cancelled, the product was 0.
(B), you found the factors of $y^2 - 3y - 18$ as $(y + 6)(y + 3)$.
(D), you failed to see that 2 is a factor in the denominator.

18. (A) Factor each term if you can.

$$\frac{x^2 - 16}{2} \div \frac{2x - 8}{6}$$

$$\frac{(x + 4)(x - 4)}{2} \div \frac{2(x - 4)}{6}$$

$$\frac{(x + 4)\cancel{(x - 4)}^1}{\cancel{2}_1} \cdot \frac{\cancel{6}^3}{2\cancel{(x - 4)}_1} = \frac{3}{2}(x + 4)$$

If your choice was
(B), you did not invert the divisor before multiplying.
(C), you cancelled $x + 4$ and $x - 4$.
(D), you inverted the dividend instead of the divisor.

19. (B) Factor each term if you can.

$$\frac{y^2 - 9}{2y + 6} \div \frac{y - 3}{y + 2}$$

$$\frac{\cancel{(y + 3)}^1\cancel{(y - 3)}^1}{2\cancel{(y + 3)}_1} \cdot \frac{y + 2}{\cancel{y - 3}_1} = \frac{y + 2}{2}$$

If your choice was
(A), you did not invert the divisor before multiplying
(C), you failed to see that 2 is a factor in the denominator.
(D), you divided the 2's in $\frac{y + 2}{2}$, and $\frac{y + 2}{2} \neq y + 1$.

20. (D) Factor each term of the fraction.

$$\frac{2x - 10}{x^2 - 25} = \frac{2\cancel{(x - 5)}^1}{\cancel{(x - 5)}_1(x + 5)} = \frac{2}{x + 5}$$

If your choice was
(A), you divided 10 and 25 by 5.
(B), you cancelled $x - 5$ and $x + 5$.
(C), you divided x and x^2 by x, and 10 and 25 by 5. The numerator is then $2 - 2$, or 0.

EQUATIONS

1. (B)
$$4x + 3 = 2x + 4$$
Subtract $2x$ from both sides of the equation.
$$2x + 3 = 4$$
Subtract 3 from both sides of the equation.
$$2x = 1$$
Divide both sides of the equation by 2.
$$x = \frac{1}{2}$$

If your choice was
(A, C, or D), see the solution above.

2. (D)
$$5(y - 2) = 3y + 4$$
First, remove the parentheses.
$$5y - 10 = 3y + 4$$
Subtract $3y$ from both sides of the equation.
$$2y - 10 = 4$$
Add 10 to both sides of the equation.
$$2y = 14$$
Divide both sides of the equation by 2.
$$y = 7$$

If your choice was
(A), you removed the parentheses incorrectly and then
  subtracted 2 from both sides of the equation:
  $5(y - 2) \neq 5y - 2$.
(B), you added $3y$ to both sides of the equation.
(C), see (A) above.

3. (C)
$$dy - c = a$$
Add c to both sides. $\quad dy = a + c$
Divide both sides by d. $\quad y = \frac{a + c}{d}$

If your choice was
(A), you failed to insert the plus sign between a and c.
(B), you divided only c by d.
(D), you inverted the answer.

4. (B) $x^2 - 5x + 6 = 0$ is a quadratic equation. Factor the
expression $x^2 - 5x + 6$.
$$x^2 - 5x + 6 = 0$$
$$(x - 3)(x - 2) = 0$$
So, $\qquad x - 3 = 0 \quad$ or $\quad x - 2 = 0$
$$x = 3 \qquad\qquad x = 2$$

If your choice was
(A), you factored $x^2 - 5x + 6$ into $(x - 1)(x - 6)$.
(C), you factored $x^2 - 5x + 6$ into $(x - 1)(x + 6)$.
(D), you factored $x^2 - 5x + 6$ into $(x - 3)(x + 2)$.

5. **(B)** Substitute 3 for y in $x = y - 3$ to get $x = 3 - 3 = 0$.

If your choice was
(A), you incorrectly added 3 and -3.
(C), see (A) above.
(D), you multiplied 3 by -3.

6. **(D)** Substitute $y - 3$ for x in the equation $y = 3x + 1$.
$$y = 3x + 1$$
$$y = 3(y - 3) + 1$$
$$y = 3y - 9 + 1$$
$$y = 3y - 8$$
$$-2y = -8$$
$$y = 4$$

If your choice was
(A), you solved $y = 3y - 8$ by adding $-3y$ to both sides but got $2y = -8$.
(B), you incorrectly multiplied $3(y - 3)$ as $3y - 3$, and then solved $y = 3y - 2$ by adding $-3y$ to both sides and got $2y = -2$.
(C), you incorrectly multiplied $3(y - 3)$ as $3y - 3$.

7. **(A)** Multiply by 2 using the distributive property.
$$3z = 2(5 - z)$$
$$3z = 10 - 2z$$
$$5z = 10$$
$$z = 2$$

If your choice was
(B), you multiplied $2(5 - z)$ as $10 - z$.
(C), see (B) above, and then you solved $3z = 10 - z$ by subtracting z from both sides.
(D), you solved $3z = 10 - 2z$ by subtracting $2z$ from both sides.

8. **(B)** Divide both sides of the equation by 2.
$$2x^2 = 72$$
$$x^2 = 36$$
$x^2 = 36$ is a quadratic equation, so set the equation equal to 0.
$$x^2 - 36 = 0$$
Factor the expression $x^2 - 36$ using the difference of two squares.
$$(x + 6)(x - 6) = 0$$
Since the product of the two factors is zero, then one of the factors is zero or both factors are zero.
So, $x + 6 = 0$ or $x - 6 = 0$
$$x = -6 \qquad x = 6$$
Therefore, the positive root is 6.

If your choice was
(A), you found the negative root.
(C), you factored $x^2 - 36$ as $(x - 18)$ and $(x + 18)$.
(D), you squared 36 instead of finding the square root.

9. (B) Substitute $2x$ for y in $x + y = 6$.
$$x + (2x) = 6$$
$$3x = 6$$
$$x = 2$$

If your choice was
(A), you solved for x in $x + y = 6$ and substituted $6 - y$ for x
  in $y = 2x$. Then you multiplied $y = 2(6 - y)$ as $y = 12 - y$.
(C), you solved $3y = 6$ as $x = 3$.
(D), you solved for y instead of for x.

10. (C)
$$a + bx = c$$
Subtract a from both sides. $\quad a + bx - a = c - a$
Divide by b. $\qquad\qquad\qquad bx = c - a$
$$x = \frac{c - a}{b}$$

If your choice was
(A), you only divided c by b.
(B), you multiplied c by a instead of subtracting.
(D), you only divided a by b when you solved $bx = c - a$.

11. (D) If
$$2x - y = 7$$
then,
$$2x - y + y = 7 + y$$
$$2x = 7 + y$$
$$2x - 7 = 7 + y - 7$$
$$2x - 7 = y$$

If your choice was
(A), you solved $2x = 7 + y$ by adding 7 to both sides.
(B), you solved $2x - y = 7$ for $-y$.
(C), you incorrectly combined 7 and $2x$.

12. (A)
$$\frac{5}{y} + 3y = \frac{17}{y}$$
Multiply both sides by y. $\quad y\left(\frac{5}{y} + 3y\right) = y\left(\frac{17}{y}\right)$
$$5 + 3y^2 = 17$$
$$3y^2 = 12$$
$$y^2 = 4$$
$$y^2 - 4 = 0$$
$$(y + 2)(y - 2) = 0$$
$$y + 2 = 0 \quad \text{or} \quad y - 2 = 0$$
$$y = -2 \qquad\qquad y = 2$$

If your choice was
(B), you found only the negative root.
(C), you found only the positive root.
(D), you divided the left side by 3 and subtracted 3 from the
  right side. Thus, $3y^2 = 12$ became $y^2 = 9$.

13. (C) Multiply both sides of the equation by 100.

Therefore, $100(0.03c) = 100(6)$

$$3c = 600$$
$$c = 200$$

If your choice was
(A), you did not multiply 6 by 100.
(B), you multiplied $0.03c$ by 100 and 6 by 10.
(D), you multiplied $0.03c$ by 100 and 6 by 1000.

14. (C) Substitute $9 - 2x$ for $3y$ in $4x - 3y = 15$.

$$4x - (9 - 2x) = 15$$
$$4x - 9 + 2x = 15$$
$$6x - 9 = 15$$
$$6x = 24$$
$$x = 4$$

If your choice was
(A), you solved $6x - 9 = 15$ by subtracting 9 from both sides.
(B), you removed the parentheses incorrectly and then solved
  $4x - 9 - 2x = 15$ by subtracting 9 from both sides.
(D), you removed the parentheses incorrectly.

15. (B) Substitute $5y$ for x in $9y + 10 - x = 12$.

$$9y + 10 - 5y = 12$$
$$4y + 10 = 12$$
$$4y = 2$$
$$y = \tfrac{1}{2}$$

If your choice was
(A), you combined $9y$ and $-5y$ as $14y$.
(C), see (A) above, and then you added 10 to both sides
  when solving $14y + 10 = 12$.
(D), you added 10 to both sides when solving $4y + 10 = 12$.

16. (D) Test each of the given choices to see which pair of numbers do
not satisfy the equation.

$$3x - 2y = 4$$

$(3, 2\tfrac{1}{2})$ $3(3) - 2\left(2\tfrac{1}{2}\right) \stackrel{?}{=} 4$

$9 - 2\left(\tfrac{5}{2}\right) \stackrel{?}{=} 4$

$9 - 5 \stackrel{?}{=} 4$

$4 = 4$ True

$(-2, -5)$ $3(-2) - 2(-5) \stackrel{?}{=} 4$

$-6 + 10 \stackrel{?}{=} 4$

$4 = 4$ True

$(4, 4)$ $3(4) - 2(4) \stackrel{?}{=} 4$

$12 - 8 \stackrel{?}{=} 4$

$4 = 4$ True

$(-2, 0)$ $3(-2) - 2(0) \stackrel{?}{=} 4$

$-6 - 0 \stackrel{?}{=} 4$

$-6 \neq 4$ False

17. **(C)** If a point lies on the graph of $x + 3y = 13$, then the coordinate pair satisfies the equation. Test each of the given choices.

$$x + 3y = 13$$

(4, −3)
$$4 + 3(-3) \stackrel{?}{=} 13$$
$$4 - 9 \stackrel{?}{=} 13$$
$$-5 \neq 13 \qquad \text{False}$$

(4, 4)
$$4 + 3(4) \stackrel{?}{=} 13$$
$$4 + 12 \stackrel{?}{=} 13$$
$$16 \neq 13 \qquad \text{False}$$

(−5, 6)
$$-5 + 3(6) \stackrel{?}{=} 13$$
$$-5 + 18 \stackrel{?}{=} 13$$
$$13 = 13 \qquad \text{True}$$

(−2, 3)
$$-2 + 3(3) \stackrel{?}{=} 13$$
$$-2 + 9 \stackrel{?}{=} 13$$
$$7 \neq 13 \qquad \text{False}$$

18. **(B)** The point $(7, a)$ lies on the graph of the equation $2x + 5y = 4$, so $(7, a)$ satisfies the equation.

$$2x + 5y = 4$$
$$2(7) + 5(a) = 4$$
$$14 + 5a = 4$$
$$5a = -10$$
$$a = -2$$

If your choice was
(A), you substituted 7 for y and a for x.
(C), you added 14 to both sides of the equation $14 + 5a = 4$.
(D), see (A) above, and then you added 35 to both sides of the equation $2a + 35 = 4$.

19. **(A)** Multiply both sides of the equation by the LCM, 15.

$$15\left(\tfrac{2t}{5} - 4\right) = 15\left(\tfrac{2t}{3}\right)$$
$$6t - 60 = 10t$$
$$-60 = 4t$$
$$-15 = t$$

If your choice was
(B), you added $6t$ to both sides of the equation $6t - 60 = 10t$.
(C), you multiplied $15\left(\tfrac{2t}{5} - 4\right)$ and got $6t - 4$.
(D), you solved $6t - 60 = 10t$ and got $-60 = -4t$.

20. (C) If the point lies on the graph of an equation, then it satisfies the equation. Test the point for each equation.

$$3x + y = 5$$
$$3(2) + (-1) \stackrel{?}{=} 5$$
$$6 - 1 \stackrel{?}{=} 5$$
$$5 = 5 \text{ True}$$

$$2x + y = 3$$
$$2(2) + (-1) \stackrel{?}{=} 3$$
$$4 - 1 \stackrel{?}{=} 3$$
$$3 = 3 \text{ True}$$

$$4x - y = 6$$
$$4(2) - (-1) \stackrel{?}{=} 6$$
$$8 + 1 \stackrel{?}{=} 6$$
$$9 \neq 6 \text{ False}$$

$$2x - y = 5$$
$$2(2) - (-1) \stackrel{?}{=} 5$$
$$4 + 1 \stackrel{?}{=} 5$$
$$5 = 5 \text{ True}$$

RATIO AND PROPORTION

1. (A) In a proportion, the product of the means is equal to the product of the extremes.

If

$$\frac{x + 1}{8} = \frac{9}{24}$$

then,

$$24(x + 1) = 8(9)$$
$$24x + 24 = 72$$
$$24x = 48$$
$$x = 2$$

If your choice was
(B), you multiplied $24(x + 1)$ and got $24x + 1$.
(C), you multiplied $9(x + 1)$ and $8(24)$.
(D), see the solution above.

2. (C) Write and solve the following proportion.

$$\frac{20}{100} = \frac{18}{x}$$
$$20x = 1800$$
$$x = 90$$

If your choice was
(A), you found 20 percent of 18.
(B), you found 200 percent of a number.
(D), you found 2 percent of a number.

3. (C) Write the following proportion.

$$\frac{x}{25} = \frac{y}{75}$$

Solve for y.

$$25y = 75x$$
$$y = 3x$$

If your choice was
(A), you wrote and solved the proportion $\frac{x}{75} = \frac{y}{25}$.

(B), you wrote and solved the proportion $\frac{x}{25} = \frac{75}{y}$.
(D), see the solution above.

4. (B) Write and solve the following proportion.

$$\frac{\text{inches}}{\text{feet}} = \frac{\text{inches}}{\text{feet}}$$

$$\frac{\frac{1}{2}}{3} = \frac{x}{24}$$

$$3x = 12$$

$$x = 4$$

If your choice was
(A), you wrote and solved the proportion $\frac{\frac{1}{2}}{24} = \frac{x}{3}$.

(C), you wrote and solved the proportion $\frac{\frac{1}{2}}{3} = \frac{24}{x}$.

(D), see the solution above.

5. (B) Write and solve the following proportion.

$$\frac{\text{girl's height}}{\text{tree's height}} = \frac{\text{girl's shadow}}{\text{tree's shadow}}$$

$$\frac{5}{30} = \frac{4}{t}$$

$$5t = 120$$

$$t = 24$$

If your choice was
(A), you wrote and solved the proportion $\frac{5}{30} = \frac{t}{4}$.

(C), you wrote and solved the proportion $\frac{5}{4} = \frac{t}{30}$.
(D), see the solution above.

6. (B) Let n = the smaller number
$5n$ = the larger number

$$n + 5n = 54$$

$$6n = 54$$

$$n = 9$$

If your choice was
(A or C), see the solution above.
(D), you found the larger number.

7. (A) Write the following proportion and solve for f.

$$\frac{\text{feet}}{\text{inches}} = \frac{\text{feet}}{\text{inches}}$$

$$\frac{f}{a} = \frac{1}{12}$$

$$12f = a$$

$$f = \frac{a}{12}$$

If your choice was
(B), you wrote and solved the proportion $\frac{f}{1} = \frac{12}{a}$.

(C), you wrote and solved the proportion $\frac{f}{a} = \frac{12}{1}$.

(D), you changed 12 feet to 36 feet by multiplying by 3.

8. (D) Write the following proportion and solve for y.

$$\frac{\text{pounds}}{\text{cents}} = \frac{\text{pounds}}{\text{cents}}$$

$$\frac{a}{b} = \frac{x}{y}$$

$$ay = bx$$

$$y = \frac{bx}{a}$$

If your choice was
(A), you used the proportion $\frac{a}{b} = \frac{y}{x}$.

(B), you used the proportion $\frac{y}{a} = \frac{1}{bx}$.

(C), you used the proportion $\frac{y}{b} = \frac{1}{ax}$.

9. (C) Write and solve the following proportion.

$$\frac{\text{inches}}{\text{miles}} = \frac{\text{inches}}{\text{miles}}$$

$$\frac{1}{60} = \frac{2\frac{1}{2}}{z}$$

$$z = 60 \cdot \frac{5}{2}$$

$$z = 150$$

If your choice was
(A), you used the proportion $\frac{1}{60} = \frac{z}{2\frac{1}{2}}$.

(B), you used the proportion $\frac{1}{2\frac{1}{2}} = \frac{z}{60}$.

(D), see the solution above.

10. (D) If

$$\frac{y}{9} = \frac{y+1}{12}$$

then,

$$12y = 9(y+1)$$
$$12y = 9y + 9$$
$$3y = 9$$
$$y = 3$$

If your choice was
(A), you multiplied $9(y+1)$ and got $9y + 1$. Then you added $9y$ to both sides of $12y = 9y + 1$.
(B), you multiplied $9(y+1)$ and got $9y + 1$.
(C), you added $9y$ to both sides of $12y = 9y + 9$.

11. (B) Write and solve the following proportion.

$$\frac{20}{100} = \frac{8}{x}$$

$$20x = 800$$
$$x = 40$$

If your choice was
(A), you found 20% of 8.
(C), you used the proportion $\frac{20}{x} = \frac{8}{100}$.
(D), see the solution above.

12. (A) Write the following proportion and solve for *x*.

$$\frac{\text{dollars}}{\text{hour}} = \frac{\text{dollars}}{\text{hour}}$$

$$\frac{d+5}{1} = \frac{x}{h}$$

$$x = h(d+5)$$

If your choice was
(B), you used the proportion $\frac{d+5}{1} = \frac{h}{x}$.

(C), you used the proportion $\frac{d+5}{h} = \frac{x}{1}$.

(D), see the solution above.

13. (D) Represent the percent of games the team won by *n*%.

Then, $\qquad \frac{25}{40} = \frac{n}{100}$

$$40n = 2500$$

$$n = 62\frac{1}{2}$$

If your choice was
(A or C), see the solution above.
(B), you found the percent of games the team lost.

14. (C)

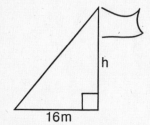 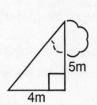

16m   4m   5m

Write and solve the following proportion.

$$\frac{\text{height}}{\text{shadow}} = \frac{\text{height}}{\text{shadow}}$$

$$\frac{h}{16} = \frac{5}{4}$$

$$4h = 80$$

$$h = 20$$

If your choice was
(A), you used the proportion $\frac{h}{16} = \frac{4}{5}$.

(B), you used the proportion $\frac{h}{5} = \frac{4}{16}$.

(D), see the solution above.

15. (A) Write and solve the following proportion.

$$\frac{\text{inches}}{\text{feet}} = \frac{\text{inches}}{\text{feet}}$$

$$\frac{y}{3x-2} = \frac{12}{1}$$

$$y = 12(3x-2)$$

$$y = 36x - 24$$

If your choice was
(B), you multiplied $12(3x - 2)$ as $36x - 2$.

(C), you used the proportion $\frac{y}{12} = \frac{1}{3x - 2}$.

(D), you used the proportion $\frac{y}{3x - 2} = \frac{1}{12}$.

16. (B) Represent the total number of tickets sold by x. Write and solve the following proportion.

$$\frac{16}{x} = \frac{25}{100}$$
$$25x = 1600$$
$$x = 64$$

If your choice was
(A), you used the proportion $\frac{x}{16} = \frac{25}{100}$.

(C), you used the proportion $\frac{25}{x} = \frac{16}{100}$.

(D), see the solution above.

17. (D) Represent the percent of students who passed the examination by $n\%$.

Then,

$$\frac{24}{30} = \frac{n}{100}$$
$$30n = 2400$$
$$n = 80$$

If your choice was
(A), you found the percent of students who failed the examination.

(B), you used the proportion $\frac{6}{24} = \frac{n}{100}$.

(C), you used the proportion $\frac{18}{24} = \frac{n}{100}$.

18. (D) If

$$\frac{x + 5}{8} = \frac{x - 1}{4}$$

then,

$$4(x + 5) = 8(x - 1)$$
$$4x + 20 = 8x - 8$$
$$28 = 4x$$
$$7 = x$$

If your choice was
(A), you multiplied $4(x + 5)$ as $4x + 5$ and $8(x - 1)$ as $8x - 1$.

(B), you multiplied $4(x + 5)$ as $4x + 5$.

(C), you multiplied $8(x - 1)$ as $8x - 1$.

19. (C) If

$$\frac{5}{x} = \frac{x}{20}$$

then,

$$x^2 = 100$$
$$x^2 - 100 = 0$$
$$(x - 10)(x + 10) = 0$$
$$x - 10 = 0 \quad \text{or} \quad x + 10 = 0$$
$$x = 10 \qquad\qquad x = -10$$

If your choice was
(A), you found only the positive root.
(B), you found only the negative root.
(D), you thought that 100 was 50^2.

20. (A) If $xy = wz$, then either pair of terms can be the means and the other the extremes.

Thus, $\frac{x}{w} = \frac{z}{y}$ or $\frac{x}{z} = \frac{w}{y}$.

Test each of the other choices:

$\frac{x}{z} = \frac{y}{w} \longrightarrow xw = yz$ False

$\frac{x}{y} = \frac{w}{z} \longrightarrow xz = yw$ False

$\frac{x}{y} = \frac{z}{w} \longrightarrow xw = yz$ False

PROBABILITY

1. (D)

Penny	Dime	Outcome
Head	Head	(H, H)
Head	Tail	(H, T)
Tail	Head	(T, H)
Tail	Tail	(T, T)

If your choice was
(A, B, or C), see the solution above.

2. (B) The two-digit numbers are as follows:

35	53	73
37	57	75

If your choice was
(A), you omitted the second possibility in 35, 53, and 73;
    for example, 37, 57, and 75.
(C), you included 33, 55, and 77.
(D), you included three-digit numbers.

3. (B) The number of three-letter outcomes beginning with *g* is 6:
gat, gae, gea, get, gta, gte
There will be 6 more for each of the starting letters *a*, *t*, and *e*, making 24 outcomes in all.

If your choice was
(A), you found the number of two-letter outcomes.
(C), you included outcomes with the same letters.
(D), you also included four-letter outcomes.

4. (C) Designate the boys as b_1, b_2, b_3, and b_4.
Designate the girls as g_1 and g_2.
The outcomes are b_1g_1, b_1g_2, b_2g_1, b_2g_2, b_3g_1, b_3g_2, b_4g_1, b_4g_2.

If your choice was
(A), you found only half of the outcomes. See solution above.
(B), you found all the possible outcomes of 2 boys or 2 girls.
(D), you found all the possible outcomes of 4 boys and 2 girls.

5. (C) The sum of 8 will appear as follows:

(2, 6), (3, 5), (4, 4), (5, 3), (6, 2)

If your choice was
(A), you tossed only one die and 8 can never be a sum.
(B), you forgot to include (4, 4).
(D), you included (4, 4) twice.

6. (B) The sum of the probability of an event's happening and the probability of an event's not happening is 1.

Thus, $1 - \frac{3}{7} = \frac{4}{7}$.

If your choice was
(A), you found the ratio of the number of favorable outcomes to the number of unfavorable outcomes.
(C), you found the ratio of the number of unfavorable outcomes to the number of favorable outcomes.
(D), $\frac{3}{7} + \frac{3}{7} \neq 1$.

7. (A) The probability (P) of an event $= \frac{\text{number of favorable outcomes}}{\text{total number of outcomes}}$.

The number of ways a sum of 12 can occur is (6, 6) or one way. Since each of the faces of one die can be associated with any of the 6 faces of the other die, the total number of possible ways is $6 \cdot 6$ or 36 ways.

Thus, $P = \frac{1}{36}$.

If your choice was
(B), you used the total number of ways 1 die can be tossed.
(C), you used (6, 6) twice as the number of favorable ways.
(D), you found the probability of *not* obtaining a sum of 12.

8. (B) Two coins can be tossed a total of four different ways: HH, HT, TH, and TT. There are two ways of tossing one head and one tail.

Therefore, $P = \frac{2}{4} = \frac{1}{2}$.

If your choice was
(A), you considered HT and TH as one way.
(C), see the solution above.
(D), you failed to see all the outcomes.

9. (C) A blouse can be chosen in 5 ways and a pair of slacks can be chosen in 3 ways. Therefore, the blouses and slacks can be arranged in 5×3 or 15 ways.

If your choice was
(A), you subtracted instead of multiplying.
(B), you added instead of multiplying.
(D), you divided instead of multiplying.

10. (D) There are 5 choices for the first place, 4 choices for the second place, 3 choices for the third place, 2 choices for the fourth place, and 1 choice for the fifth place. Therefore, there are $5 \times 4 \times 3 \times 2 \times 1$ or 120 different ways that the five students can be arranged in a row.

> *If your choice was*
> (A or C), see the solution above.
> (B), you added instead of multiplying.

11. (B) There are 13 hearts in an ordinary deck of cards. Therefore, $P = \frac{13}{52} = \frac{1}{4}$.

> *If your choice was*
> (A), you thought that there was 1 heart in the deck.
> (C), you found the probability of *not* choosing a heart.
> (D), see (A) above. Then you found the probability of *not* choosing a heart.

12. (B) There are 3 red buttons out of a total of 10 buttons. Therefore, $P = \frac{3}{10}$.

> *If your choice was*
> (A), you found the probability of drawing a green button.
> (C), you found the probability of drawing a yellow button.
> (D), you thought that drawing a red button is a certainty.

13. (C) Mr. Sweeney has 12 chances out of 6000 chances to win the car, or $P = \frac{12}{6000} = \frac{1}{500}$. The probability that Mr. Sweeney will *not* win is $1 - \frac{1}{500}$ or $\frac{499}{500}$.

> *If your choice was*
> (A), you are ruling out any probability that he will win even though he bought 12 chances.
> (B), you found the probability of his winning.
> (D), you think he will definitely win even though 5988 chances were sold to others.

14. (D) The vowels are a, e, i, o, and u. Therefore, there are 3 vowels out of 6 letters. The probability is $P = \frac{3}{6} = \frac{1}{2}$.

> *If your choice was*
> (A), you did not know a, e, and u were vowels.
> (B), you thought there was only 1 vowel.
> (C), you thought there were only 2 vowels.

15. (B) There are 4 jacks, 4 queens, and 4 kings. Therefore, $P = \frac{12}{52} = \frac{3}{13}$.

If your choice was
(A), you forgot there are 4 of each card.
(C), you found the probability that it will *not* be either a jack, a queen, or a king.
(D), you thought that choosing a jack, a queen, or a king was a certainty.

16. (A) There are 2 red marbles and 3 yellow marbles out of 9 marbles in all. The number of favorable ways is $2 + 3 = 5$. The total number of ways is $2 + 4 + 3 = 9$.
Thus, $P = \frac{5}{9}$.

If your choice was
(B), you found the probability of picking a red or a blue marble.
(C), you found the probability of picking a blue or a yellow marble.
(D), you found the probability of picking only a red marble.

17. (B) The sum of the probability of winning and of not winning is 1. Therefore, $1 - 0.6 = 0.4$.

If your choice was
(A, C, or D), see the solution above.

18. (C) There are 4 choices for the first digit, 3 choices for the second digit, 2 choices for the third digit, and 1 choice for the fourth digit. Therefore, $4 \times 3 \times 2 \times 1$ or 24 different arrangements of four digits can be made.

If your choice was
(A), you only found one of the possible arrangements for each numeral beginning with 2, 5, 6, and 8.
(B), see the solution above.
(D), you included 2222, 5555, 6666, and 8888 in your solution.

19. (A) There is no way to obtain 9¢ by drawing two coins from the box. Therefore, the probability is 0.

If your choice was
(B), you found the probability that the sum of the two coins is 2¢.
(C), you found the probability that the sum of the two coins is 15¢.
(D), see the solution above.

20. (D) A lunch consists of a sandwich and a fruit. There are 6 different sandwiches from which to choose but nothing is said about the different fruits. So, the answer cannot be determined from the information given.

If your choice was
(A, B, or C), see the solution above.

INEQUALITIES

1. (B) Test each of the given choices with $a = -3$.

If $a + 1 > 0$, then $-3 + 1 \overset{?}{>} 0$ or $-2 \not> 0$. False

If $a - 3 < 0$, then $-3 - 3 \overset{?}{<} 0$ or $-6 < 0$. True

If $a^2 < a$, then $(-3)^2 \overset{?}{<} -3$ or $9 \not< -3$. False

If $2a > 0$, then $2(-3) \overset{?}{>} 0$ or $-6 \not> 0$. False

2. (D) If x is greater than y, which is greater than z, then x must be greater than z. Test each of the other choices using $x = -2$, $y = -3$, and $z = -4$.

If your choice was
(A), $xy > yz$ gives $6 \not> 12$. False
(B), $xyz > 0$ gives $-24 \not> 0$. False
(C), $x + y > z$ gives $-5 \not> -4$. False

3. (A) Add $-2 - x$ to both sides of the inequality.
$$2 + 3x > x - 4$$
$$2 + 3x - 2 - x > x - 4 - 2 - x$$
$$2x > -6$$
$$x > -3$$

If your choice was
(B), you added 2 to the right side of the inequality and subtracted 2 from the left side.
(C), you added x to the left side of the inequality and subtracted x from the right side.
(D), you added $-2 + x$ to the left side of the inequality and $2 - x$ to the right side.

4. (D) If $a > b$, then it follows that $3a > 3b$. Test each of the other choices using $a = -2$ and $b = -3$.

If your choice was
(A), $a - b < 0$ gives $-2 - (-3) \overset{?}{<} 0$ or
$1 \not< 0$. False
(B), $a^2 > b^2$ gives $4 \not> 9$. False
(C), $ab > 0$ gives $6 > 0$. True. Then try
$a = 6$ and $b = -3$. Then $-18 \not> 0$. False

5. (C) The given relationship means that x is greater than -6 but less than or equal to -2.

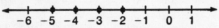

Thus, x consists of all integers greater than but not including -6 and less than and including -2.

If your choice was
(A or B), you included -6.
(D), see the solution above.

6. (A) Add $+4$ to both sides of the inequality.

$$1 < 3x - 4$$
$$1 + 4 < 3x - 4 + 4$$
$$5 < 3x$$
$$\tfrac{5}{3} < x \ \text{ or } \ x > \tfrac{5}{3}$$

If your choice was
(B), you reversed the inequality sign.
(C), you added -4 to the left side and added $+4$ to the right side.
(D), see (B) and (C) above.

7. (C) If a pair of coordinates represents an element of the solution set, then the pair of coordinates must satisfy the inequality. Therefore, substitute 1 for x and k for y.

$$x + 3y < 7$$
$$1 + 3k < 7$$
$$1 + 3k - 1 < 7 - 1$$
$$3k < 6$$
$$k < 2$$

Thus, k must have a value less than 2. The only choice is (C), k could be 1.

If your choice was
(A, B, or D), see the solution above.

8. (B) Add $+3x - 2$ to both sides of the inequality.

$$2 - 3x < x + 2$$
$$2 - 3x + 3x - 2 < x + 2 + 3x - 2$$
$$0 < 4x$$
$$0 < x \ \text{ or } \ x > 0$$

If your choice was
(A), you reversed the inequality sign.
(C), you added $-3x + 2$ to both sides and got $4 < 4x$ or $x > 1$.
(D), see (C) above. Then you reversed the inequality sign.

9. (D) The open circle at -2 indicates that -2 is not included in the solution set. The closed circle at 1 indicates that 1 is included in the solution set. Therefore, the graph is the set of numbers greater than -2 and less than or equal to 1, or $-2 < x \le 1$.

If your choice was
(A), you included -2 in the solution set.
(B), see (A) above and you left 1 out of the solution set.
(C), you left 1 out of the solution set.

10. (A) Add −1 to both sides of the inequality.

$$3y + 1 \leq 10$$
$$3y + 1 - 1 \leq 10 - 1$$
$$3y \leq 9$$
$$y \leq 3$$

All values of y must be less than or equal to 3. The largest value of y is 3.

If your choice was
(B or D), you did not find the largest value of y.
(C), see the solution above.

11. (B) The given relationship means that x is greater than or equal to −3 but less than 2. Thus, −3 is included in the solution set and should be indicated on the graph by a closed circle. An open circle should be at 2 since 2 is not included in the solution set. The only graph with both conditions is B.

If your choice was
(A), you included 2 in the solution set.
(C), you did not include −3 in the solution set.
(D), see (A) and (C) above.

12. (C) If

$$8x \geq 3(x - 5)$$

then,

$$8x \geq 3x - 15$$
$$5x \geq -15$$
$$x \geq -3$$

If your choice was
(A), you left out $x = -3$.
(B), you multiplied $3(x - 5)$ as $3x - 5$ and deleted $x = -1$.
(D), you multiplied $3(x - 5)$ as $3x - 5$.

13. (D) The coordinates $(2, k)$ must satisfy the inequality, so substitute 2 for x and k for y.

$$y > -2x + 7$$
$$k > -2(2) + 7$$
$$k > -4 + 7$$
$$k > 3$$

Thus, k must have a value greater than 3. The only choice is (D), k could be 5.

If your choice was
(A, B, or C), see the solution above.

14. (C) Use the distributive property to remove the parentheses.

$$3(3x + 2) > 2(x + 8)$$
$$9x + 6 > 2x + 16$$

Add $-2x - 6$ to both sides of the inequality.

$$9x + 6 - 2x - 6 > 2x + 16 - 2x - 6$$
$$7x > 10$$
$$x > \frac{10}{7} \text{ or } 1\frac{3}{7}$$

If your choice was
(A), you multiplied $2(x + 8)$ as $2x + 8$.
(B), you multiplied $3(3x + 2)$ as $9x + 2$ and see (A) above.
(D), you multiplied $3(3x + 2)$ as $9x + 2$.

15. (A) Test each of the given choices in the given inequality.
$$x^2 + 4x < 0$$

(A) $x > 0$. Try $x = 1$. $1^2 + 4(1) \overset{?}{<} $ or $5 \not< 0$. False
(B) $x > -4$. Try $x = -3$. $(-3)^2 + 4(-3) \overset{?}{<} 0$ or $-3 < 0$. True
(C) $x < 0$. Try $x = -1$. $(-1)^2 + 4(-1) \overset{?}{<} 0$ or $-3 < 0$. True
(D) $x < -1$. Try $x = -2$. $(-2)^2 + 4(-2) \overset{?}{<} 0$ or $-4 < 0$. True

16. (D) Add 5 to the entire inequality.
$$-1 < 2x - 5 \leq 3$$
$$-1 + 5 < 2x - 5 + 5 \leq 3 + 5$$
Divide by 2. $\qquad\qquad 4 < 2x \leq 8$
$$2 < x \leq 4$$
Thus, x must be either 3 or 4.

If your choice was
(A), you included 2 in the solution set.
(B), you excluded 4 from the solution set.
(C), you excluded 3 from the solution set.

17. (D) Divide both sides of the inequality by -4.
Recall that if $a > b$ and $c < 0$, then $\frac{a}{c} < \frac{b}{c}$.
Therefore, $\qquad \frac{-4x}{-4} > \frac{-8}{-4}$
$$x < 2$$

If your choice was
(A, B, or C), see the solution above.

18. (B) Add the two inequalities.
$$\begin{array}{r} a > b \\ a > c \\ \hline 2a > b + c \end{array}$$
Use $a = 1$, $b = -3$, and $c = -4$ to test the other choices.

(A) If $b < c$, then $-3 \not< -4$. False
(C) If $b - a > c$, then $-3 - 1 \overset{?}{>} -4$ or $-4 > -4$. False
(D) If $b + c > a$, then $-3 + (-4) \overset{?}{>} 1$ or $-7 \not> 1$. False

19. (C) Since $y > z$ and $z > x$, then $y > x$.
Subtract a from both sides of the inequality.
$$y > x$$
$$y - a > x - a$$
Test each of the other choices in the inequality using
$a = 2$, $x = 3$, $z = 4$, and $y = 5$.

(A) If $y < a$, then $5 \not< 2$. False
(B) If $2a > x + y$, then $2(2) \overset{?}{>} 3 + 5$ or $4 \not> 8$. False
(D) If $x > y$, then $3 \not> 5$. False

20. (A) The closed circle at -1 indicates that -1 is included in the solution set. Since the line extends to the right on the number line, all values greater than -1 are also included. Thus, $x \geq -1$.

If your choice was
(B), you failed to include -1 in the solution set.
(C), you went to the left rather than to the right on the number line.
(D), you included -1 but see (C) above.

PROBLEM SOLVING

1. (B) Let y = number of degrees in the measure of one of the equal angles

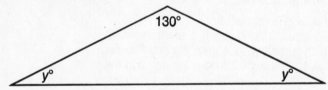

Since the sum of the degree measures of the three angles of any triangle is 180, write an equation and solve.
$$y + y + 130 = 180$$
$$2y = 50$$
$$y = 25$$

If your choice was
(A), you subtracted 130 from both sides of the equation and got $2y = 30$.
(C), you solved $y + 130 = 180$.
(D), you subtracted 30 from both sides of the equation and got $2y = 150$.

2. (B) Let $\quad n$ = 1st consecutive odd integer
$\quad n + 2$ = 2nd consecutive odd integer

Then,
$$n^2 = 3(n + 2) + 4$$
$$n^2 = 3n + 6 + 4$$
$$n^2 = 3n + 10$$
$$n^2 - 3n - 10 = 0$$
$$(n - 5)(n + 2) = 0$$
$$n - 5 = 0 \quad \text{or} \quad n + 2 = 0$$
$$n = 5 \qquad\qquad n = -2$$
$$n + 2 = 7 \qquad\qquad \text{(Reject since } n \text{ must be positive.)}$$

If your choice was
(A or D), see the solution above.
(C), you found the larger consecutive odd integer.

3. (B) Let w = the number of meters in the width
       $w + 8$ = the number of meters in the length

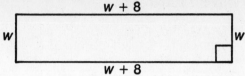

Then, $w + (w + 8) + w + (w + 8) = 56$
$$4w + 16 = 56$$
$$4w = 40$$
$$w = 10$$
$$w + 8 = 18$$

If your choice was
(A), you found the number of meters in the width.
(C), you forgot to include the 4 sides of the rectangle.
(D), you wrote w and $8w$ as the width and length.

4. (C) Let y = the length of the shorter leg
       $y + 7$ = the length of the longer leg
       $y + 9$ = the length of the hypotenuse

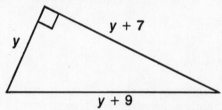

Then, $y + (y + 7) + (y + 9) = 40$
$$3y + 16 = 40$$
$$3y = 24$$
$$y = 8$$
$$y + 7 = 15$$
$$y + 9 = 17$$

If your choice was
(A), you found the length of the shorter leg.
(B), you found the length of the longer leg.
(D), you solved $3y + 16 = 40$ as $3y = 27$.

5. (A) Let x = the number of tickets sold in advance
       $100 - x$ = the number of tickets sold at the door

Then, $0.75\,(x) + 1(100 - x) = 85$
Multiply by 100. $75x + 100(100 - x) = 8500$
$$75x + 10000 - 100x = 8500$$
$$-25x = -1500$$
$$x = 60$$
$$100 - x = 40$$

If your choice was
(B), you found the number of tickets sold in advance.
(C or D), see the solution above.

6. (C) Let $\quad u = $ units digit
$t = $ tens digit
$10t + u = $ the number

Then, $\qquad\qquad\qquad 10t + u = 6(t + u)$
$$2u = t + 3$$
Simplify the first equation.
$$10t + u = 6t + 6u$$
$$4t = 5u$$
Solve the second equation for t.
$$t = 2u - 3$$
Substitute $2u - 3$ for t in the first equation.
$$4(2u - 3) = 5u$$
$$8u - 12 = 5u$$
$$3u = 12$$
$$u = 4$$
Substitute 4 for u in $t = 2u - 3$.
$$t = 2(4) - 3$$
$$t = 5$$

Thus, the number is $10t + u$ or $10(5) + 4 = 54$.

If your choice was
(A), $12 \neq 6(1 + 2)$
(B), $33 \neq 6(3 + 3)$
(D), $75 \neq 6(7 + 5)$

7. (B) Let $\;w = $ the hourly wage of the helper
$3w = $ the hourly wage of the mechanic

Then, $\qquad\qquad\qquad 5w + 4(3w) = 68$
$$5w + 12w = 68$$
$$17w = 68$$
$$w = 4$$
$$3w = 12$$

If your choice was
(A), you found the hourly wage of the helper.
(C), you used the equation $w + 3w = 68$ and
gave the hourly wage of the helper.
(D), you used the equation $w + 3w = 68$.

8. (C) Let $\qquad\qquad x = $ amount in dollars invested at 6%
$7200 - x = $ amount in dollars invested at 7%
$0.06x = $ income from 6% investment
$0.07(7200 - x) = $ income from 7% investment

Then, $\qquad 0.06x + 0.07(7200 - x) = 464$
$$6x + 7(7200 - x) = 46400$$
$$6x + 50400 - 7x = 46400$$
$$-x = -4000$$
$$x = 4000$$
$$7200 - x = 3200$$

If your choice was
(A), you found $7(7200 - x)$ as $50400 - x$ and then solved the equation incorrectly.
(B), you found the amount invested at 7%.
(D), see (A) and (B) above.

9. (D) Let
$$x = \text{the number of 22¢ stamps}$$
$$80 - x = \text{the number of 17¢ stamps}$$

Then,
$$0.22x + 0.17(80 - x) = 16.35$$
$$22x + 17(80 - x) = 1635$$
$$22x + 1360 - 17x = 1635$$
$$5x = 275$$
$$x = 55$$

If your choice was
(A), you found $17(80 - x)$ as $1360 + 17x$ and then discarded the remainder in $39x = 275$.
(B), you found $17(80 - x)$ as $1360 - x$ and discarded the remainder in $21x = 275$.
(C), you found the number of 17¢ stamps.

10. (B)

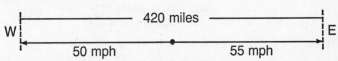

Let
$$t = \text{time in hours for the women to be 420 miles apart}$$
$$50t = \text{distance of woman traveling westward}$$
$$55t = \text{distance of woman traveling eastward}$$

Then,
$$50t + 55t = 420$$
$$105t = 420$$
$$t = 4$$

If your choice was
(A, C, or D), see the solution above.

11. (D) Let $x = $ the number of hours it takes Tom alone to paint the wall
$2x = $ the number of hours it takes Sam alone to paint the wall

	Time working alone in hours	Part of job done in 1 hour	Part of job done in 6 hours
Sam	$2x$	$\frac{1}{2x}$	$6\left(\frac{1}{2x}\right) = \frac{6}{2x} = \frac{3}{x}$
Tom	x	$\frac{1}{x}$	$6\left(\frac{1}{x}\right) = \frac{6}{x}$

Then,
$$\frac{3}{x} + \frac{6}{x} = 1$$
$$\frac{9}{x} = 1$$
$$x = 9$$
$$2x = 18$$

If your choice was

(A), you used the equation $\frac{1}{x} + \frac{1}{2x} = 6$.

(B), you used the equation $\frac{2x}{6} + \frac{x}{6} = 1$.

(C), you found the number of hours if would take Tom alone to do the job.

12. (A) Let
z = the number of each kind of coin
z = value in cents of pennies
$5z$ = value in cents of nickels
$10z$ = value in cents of dimes

Then,
$$z + 5z + 10z = 240$$
$$16z = 240$$
$$z = 15$$

If your choice was
(B,C, or D), see the solution above.

13. (D) Let
x = Jim's age now
$x + 6$ = Jane's age now
$x - 6$ = Jim's age 6 years ago
$(x + 6) - 6$ = Jane's age 6 years ago

Then,
$$(x + 6) - 6 = 2(x - 6)$$
$$x + 6 - 6 = 2x - 12$$
$$x = 2x - 12$$
$$12 = x$$
$$18 = x + 6$$

If your choice was
(A), you used the equation $x + 6 = 2x$ and found Jim's age.
(B), you solved $x = 2x - 12$ as $3x = 12$.
(C), you found Jim's age.

14. (A) Let
x = the number of degrees in the measure of the second angle
$2x$ = the number of degrees in the measure of the first angle
$x + 20$ = the number of degrees in the measure of the third angle

Then,
$$x + 2x + (x + 20) = 180$$
$$4x + 20 = 180$$
$$4x = 160$$
$$x = 40$$
$$2x = 80$$
$$x + 20 = 60$$

If your choice was
(B), you added 20 to the right side of $4x + 20 = 180$ and subtracted 20 from the left side.
(C), you found the measure of the third angle.
(D), you found the measure of the first angle.

15. **(C)** Let y = the smaller positive number
$y + 2$ = the larger positive number

Then,
$$y^2 + (y + 2)^2 = 34$$
$$y^2 + y^2 + 4y + 4 = 34$$
$$2y^2 + 4y - 30 = 0$$
$$y^2 + 2y - 15 = 0$$
$$(y + 5)(y - 3) = 0$$
$$y + 5 = 0 \quad \text{or} \quad y - 3 = 0$$
$$y = -5 \qquad\qquad y = 3$$
$$\text{(Reject)} \qquad y + 2 = 5$$

If your choice was
(A), you found the smaller negative number.
(B), you found the larger negative number.
(D), you found the larger positive number.

16. **(A)** Let n = the 1st consecutive integer
$n + 1$ = the 2nd consecutive integer
$n + 2$ = the 3rd consecutive integer

Then,
$$n + (n + 1) + (n + 2) < 86$$
$$3n + 3 < 86$$
$$3n < 83$$
$$n < 27\tfrac{2}{3}$$

Thus, 27 is the smallest consecutive integer.

If your choice was
(B), you found the 2nd consecutive integer
(C), you found the 3rd consecutive integer.
(D), see the solution above.

17. **(A)** Let n = the number of nickels
$20 - n$ = the number of quarters
$5n$ = value in cents of the nickels
$25(20 - n)$ = value in cents of the quarters

Then,
$$5n + 25(20 - n) = 440$$
$$5n + 500 - 25n = 440$$
$$-20n = -60$$
$$n = 3$$

If your choice was
(B), you multiplied $25(20 - n)$ as $500 - n$ and then solved
$4n = -60$ as $n = 15$.
(C), you did all of (B) above and then found the number of
quarters.
(D), you found the number of quarters.

18. **(A)** Let w = the width of the rectangle
$2w - 1$ = the length of the rectangle

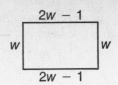

Then, $w + (2w - 1) + w + (2w - 1) = 76$

$$6w - 2 = 76$$
$$6w = 78$$
$$w = 13$$
$$2w - 1 = 2(13) - 1 = 25$$

If your choice was
(B), you found the length of the rectangle.
(C), you used the equation $w + 2(w - 1) = 76$.
(D), see (C) above and then you found the length of the rectangle.

19. (D)

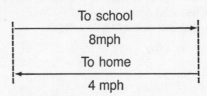

Let $t =$ the number of hours it took traveling to school
$3 - t =$ the number of hours it took traveling home
$8t =$ distance traveled to school
$4(3 - t) =$ distance traveled home

Then,
$$8t = 4(3 - t)$$
$$8t = 12 - 4t$$
$$12t = 12$$
$$t = 1$$

Thus, it is 8 miles from school to her home.

If your choice was
(A), you found the time it took to get to school.
(B), you found the time it took to return home.
(C), you used $4(1)$ to find the distance from school to her home.

20. (D) Let
$x =$ the number of student tickets sold
$850 - x =$ the number of adult tickets sold
$150x =$ receipts in cents for student tickets
$200(850 - x) =$ receipts in cents for adult tickets

Then,
$$150x + 200(850 - x) = 165000$$
$$150x + 170000 - 200x = 165000$$
$$-50x = -5000$$
$$x = 100$$
$$850 - x = 750$$

If your choice was
(A), you found the number of student tickets sold.
(B or C), see the solution above.

Part Four

Two SAT-Type Algebra Tests

This section contains two SAT-Type Algebra Tests modeled after the SAT Mathematics Section.

Use the Answer Sheet that precedes each test to record your answers. The Answer Sheet for Test 1 is found on page 138. The Answer Sheet for Test 2 is on page 152.

After you have completed each test, you can check your answers using the Answer Keys on pages 144 and 158. If you need additional help, each answer is referenced (in parentheses) to the appropriate Algebra Refresher Section.

The solutions with error analysis begin on page 145 and page 159.

Types of Multiple-Choice Questions

There are two types of multiple-choice questions used in the mathematical section of the SAT: standard multiple-choice questions and quantitative comparison questions. There are approximately twice as many standard multiple-choice questions as quantitative comparison questions on the test.

Reference Information for SAT-Type Tests

In the introduction to each section of the SAT math test, information is provided for your reference in solving some of the problems. This information appears in the test booklet. Knowledge of this information beforehand will help when you take the actual test.

Definition of symbols:

$=$ is equal to $\qquad$ $>$ is greater than
$\neq$ is unequal to $\qquad$ $\leq$ is less than or equal to
$<$ is less than $\qquad$ $\geq$ is greater than or equal to

Answer Sheet*

SAT-Type Algebra Test 1

1. Ⓐ Ⓑ Ⓒ Ⓓ Ⓔ
2. Ⓐ Ⓑ Ⓒ Ⓓ Ⓔ
3. Ⓐ Ⓑ Ⓒ Ⓓ Ⓔ
4. Ⓐ Ⓑ Ⓒ Ⓓ Ⓔ
5. Ⓐ Ⓑ Ⓒ Ⓓ Ⓔ
6. Ⓐ Ⓑ Ⓒ Ⓓ Ⓔ
7. Ⓐ Ⓑ Ⓒ Ⓓ Ⓔ
8. Ⓐ Ⓑ Ⓒ Ⓓ Ⓔ
9. Ⓐ Ⓑ Ⓒ Ⓓ Ⓔ
10. Ⓐ Ⓑ Ⓒ Ⓓ Ⓔ
11. Ⓐ Ⓑ Ⓒ Ⓓ Ⓔ
12. Ⓐ Ⓑ Ⓒ Ⓓ Ⓔ
13. Ⓐ Ⓑ Ⓒ Ⓓ Ⓔ
14. Ⓐ Ⓑ Ⓒ Ⓓ Ⓔ
15. Ⓐ Ⓑ Ⓒ Ⓓ Ⓔ
16. Ⓐ Ⓑ Ⓒ Ⓓ Ⓔ
17. Ⓐ Ⓑ Ⓒ Ⓓ Ⓔ
18. Ⓐ Ⓑ Ⓒ Ⓓ Ⓔ

19. Ⓐ Ⓑ Ⓒ Ⓓ Ⓔ
20. Ⓐ Ⓑ Ⓒ Ⓓ Ⓔ
21. Ⓐ Ⓑ Ⓒ Ⓓ Ⓔ
22. Ⓐ Ⓑ Ⓒ Ⓓ Ⓔ
23. Ⓐ Ⓑ Ⓒ Ⓓ Ⓔ
24. Ⓐ Ⓑ Ⓒ Ⓓ Ⓔ
25. Ⓐ Ⓑ Ⓒ Ⓓ Ⓔ
26. Ⓐ Ⓑ Ⓒ Ⓓ Ⓔ
27. Ⓐ Ⓑ Ⓒ Ⓓ Ⓔ
28. Ⓐ Ⓑ Ⓒ Ⓓ Ⓔ
29. Ⓐ Ⓑ Ⓒ Ⓓ Ⓔ
30. Ⓐ Ⓑ Ⓒ Ⓓ Ⓔ
31. Ⓐ Ⓑ Ⓒ Ⓓ Ⓔ
32. Ⓐ Ⓑ Ⓒ Ⓓ Ⓔ
33. Ⓐ Ⓑ Ⓒ Ⓓ Ⓔ
34. Ⓐ Ⓑ Ⓒ Ⓓ Ⓔ
35. Ⓐ Ⓑ Ⓒ Ⓓ Ⓔ

*An Answer Sheet very much like this will be given to you at the actual test. In doing the following practice test, you may wish to record your answers on this Answer Sheet. However, it may be more convenient for you to circle your answer from among the choices provided.

SAT-Type Algebra Test 1

> **Directions:**
> Solve each problem in this practice test. Use any available space on the page for scratchwork. Then decide which is the best of the choices given and either darken the corresponding space on the Answer Sheet on page 138 or circle your answer from among the choices provided.

1. If $\frac{8}{r} = 2$ and $3s + r = 19$, then $s =$

  (A) 1   (B) $6\frac{1}{4}$ (C) 2   (D) 4   (E) 5

2. If $\frac{12}{z} = \frac{3}{8}$, then $z =$

  (A) 24   (B) 28   (C) 32   (D) 36   (E) 40

3. Which of the following must be negative?

  I. The product of 2 negative numbers
  II. The product of 2 positive numbers
  III. The product of 3 negative numbers

  (A) I only   (B) II only   (C) III only
  (D) I and II only   (E) I and III only

4. If $y = 2x^2 - 3x$ and $x = 3$, then $y =$

  (A) 1   (B) 3   (C) 6   (D) 9   (E) 12

5.

	Scale I	Scale II
Freezing	0°	50°
Boiling	100°	300°

The table above shows boiling and freezing points of the same liquid measured under the same conditions on two different temperature scales. The numbers on each of the scales are equally spaced. How many degrees on Scale II would correspond to 50° on Scale I?

  (A) 100   (B) 125   (C) 150   (D) 175   (E) 200

6. If $x - y = n$ and $x + y = \frac{1}{n}, n \neq 0$, then $x^2 - y^2 =$

  (A) n (B) n^2 (C) $\frac{1}{n}$ (D) 0   (E) 1

7. $2^2 + 3^2 + (2 + 3)^2 =$

  (A) 23   (B) 35   (C) 38   (D) 49   (E) 100

8. If $y = 4$, then $\sqrt{9 - 6y + y^2} =$

   (A) -1 (B) 0 (C) 1 (D) 2 (E) 3

9. If a and b are integers, which of the following is (are) always true?

   I. $(ab)^2 = a^2b^2$
   II. $a^2 - b^2 = (a + b)(a - b)$
   III. $a^2 + b^2 = (a + b)^2$

   (A) I only   (B) II only   (C) III only
   (D) I and II only   (E) I, II, and III

10. If the ratio of e to f is $\frac{1}{3}$ and the ratio of g to h is $\frac{1}{6}$, then the ratio of $e + 2g$ to $f + h$ is

   (A) $\frac{1}{2}$ (B) $\frac{1}{4}$ (C) $\frac{5}{6}$

   (D) $\frac{1}{12}$ (E) $\frac{1}{3}$

11. If $-1 < 4x + 7 < 11$, then the values of x that will satisfy the condition are

   (A) $-2 < x < 1$ (B) $-4 < x < 1$ (C) $x < -2$ or $x > 1$
   (D) $-\frac{1}{4} < x < \frac{11}{4}$ (E) $2 > x > -1$

12. If $n - m = -3$ and $mn = 3$, then $\frac{1}{n} - \frac{1}{m} =$

   (A) -6 (B) -1 (C) 0 (D) 1 (E) 6

13. A car can travel 40 mph going uphill and 60 mph going downhill. What is its average speed, in miles per hour, if it goes 100 miles uphill and then 100 miles downhill?

   (A) 40 (B) 48 (C) 50 (D) 60 (E) $62\frac{1}{2}$

14. If $pq - p = 6$ and $\frac{1}{p} - \frac{1}{q-1} = \frac{2}{3}$, then $q - p =$

   (A) 3 (B) 4 (C) 5 (D) 6 (E) 7

15. If $(r - 1)\left(\frac{1}{r}\right) = 0$, what is r?

   (A) -2 (B) -1 (C) 1
   (D) 2 (E) Any integer

16. Which of the following conditions is necessary so that $x^2 + xy - 3x - 3y = 0$ will have $x = 3$ as one solution?

   (A) $y > 0$ (B) $x \neq y$ (C) $x \neq 0$
   (D) $y \neq 0$ (E) $x \neq -y$

Questions 17–26 each consist of two quantities, one in Column A and one in Column B. You are to compare the two quantities and on the answer sheet blacken space

A if the quantity in Column A is greater;
B if the quantity in Column B is greater;
C if the two quantities are equal;
D if the relationship cannot be determined
from the information given.

An E response will not be scored.

Notes:

1. In certain questions, information concerning one or both of the quantities to be compared is centered above the two columns.
2. In a given question, a symbol that appears in both columns represents the same thing in Column A as it does in Column B.
3. Letters such as x, n, and k stand for real numbers.

Column A	*Column B*

$$\frac{3}{4} = \frac{x}{6} \qquad \frac{6}{y} = \frac{4}{3}$$

17. x $\qquad\qquad$ y

Three times the sum of 10 and
twice some number s is 54.

18. 3 $\qquad\qquad$ s

$$y^3 + y^2 = 1$$

19. $y^2(y + 1)$ $\qquad\qquad$ 1

$$\frac{a}{b} = \frac{c}{d}$$

20. $\dfrac{a + b}{b}$ $\qquad\qquad$ $\dfrac{c + d}{d}$

$$y > 0$$

21. $x - y$ $\qquad\qquad$ positive number

$N^* = (N - 2)^2$ for all positive integers N.

22. 1^* $\qquad\qquad$ 3^*

	Column A	Column B

$$a * b = \frac{2a - b}{2b - a}$$

23. $1 * (2 * 3)$ $(1 * 2) * 3$

$$y = x^2 + 8x + 15$$

24. y when $x = -5$ y when $x = -3$

$$a > b + 1$$

25. a b

$$p > q > 0$$

26. $p^2 + q^2$ $(p + q)^2 - 2pq$

Directions:
Solve each of the remaining problems in this practice test using any available space on the page for scratchwork. Then decide which is the best of the choices given and either darken the corresponding space on the Answer Sheet on page 138 or circle your answer from among the choices provided.

27. If $w, x, y,$ and z are a series of positive numbers such that each number is twice the previous one, then which of the following must be true?

(A) $w + x + y = z$ (B) $w + y = x + z$ (C) $wy = xz$
(D) $\frac{z}{x} = \frac{y}{w}$ (E) $\frac{wx}{y} = z$

28. The sum of two prime numbers is

(A) always prime.
(B) always even.
(C) always odd.
(D) always prime if the numbers are equal.
(E) never prime if the numbers are equal.

29. If $\dfrac{\frac{x}{y}}{y} = x^2$ and $x = \frac{1}{4}$, then $y =$

(A) $\frac{1}{4}$ and $-\frac{1}{4}$ (B) $\frac{1}{2}$ and $-\frac{1}{2}$ (C) $\frac{1}{8}$ and $-\frac{1}{8}$
(D) 1 and -1 (E) 2 and -2

30. If $x \neq 0$ and $x \neq 1$, then $\frac{x}{x+1} - \frac{x-1}{x} =$

(A) $\frac{1}{x(x+1)}$ (B) 1 (C) $\frac{1}{x+1}$

(D) $-\frac{1}{x}$ (E) $\frac{-1}{x(x-1)}$

31. For all numbers x and y, where $y \neq 0$, $x * y = \frac{x - 2y^3}{y^2}$.
Then, $10^6 * 10^2 =$

(A) 80 (B) $-\frac{2}{10^3}$ (C) -10^2 (D) $-\frac{1}{10^2}$ (E) 10^2

32. If $z^2 = 2$, then $z^3 =$

(A) $-\sqrt{6}$ (B) $2\sqrt{2}$ only   (C) $-2\sqrt{2}$ only

(D) $\sqrt{6}$ (E) $2\sqrt{2}$ or $-2\sqrt{2}$

33. If y and z are two distinct positive integers and both y and z are divisible by 23, the smallest possible sum of y and z is

(A) 0 (B) 23 (C) 46 (D) 69 (E) 92

34. If $x \square y = \frac{x}{x-1} - \frac{y+1}{y}$ with $x \neq 1$ and $y \neq 0$, then the value of $3 \square 6$ is

(A) greater then $\frac{1}{2}$ (B) less than $\frac{1}{4}$

(C) equal to $\frac{1}{4}$ (D) equal to $\frac{1}{2}$

(E) greater than $\frac{1}{4}$ but less than $\frac{1}{2}$

35. A car rental company rents automobiles at a rate of d dollars per day and x cents per mile. If a car was rented for 12 days and the odometer showed an addition of 600 miles traveled, then the amount, in dollars, due the company was

(A) $6(2d + x)$ (B) $\frac{12(d + 50x)}{100}$ (C) $600(2d + x)$

(D) $12(d + 50x)$ (E) $6(d + 2x)$

Answer Key to SAT-Type Algebra Test 1

Following each answer, there is a number or numbers in the form "*a.b*" in parentheses. This number refers to the Algebra Refresher Section (beginning on page 23). The first number "*a*" indicates the section:

1. Integers	5. Ratio and Proportion
2. Algebraic Expressions	6. Probability
3. Factoring	7. Inequalities
4. Equations	8. Problem Solving

The number "*b*" indicates the part of the section that explains the rule or method used in solving the problem.

---

1. E (4.6, 4.3, 4.2)	**13.** B (8.3)	**25.** A (7.1, 2.6)
2. C (5.4, 4.3)	**14.** C (2.8, 2.6)	**26.** C (2.9, 2.8)
3. C (1.6, 1.7, 1.3)	**15.** C (4.4, 4.3)	**27.** D (8.1)
4. D (4.6, 4.3)	**16.** E (4.3, 3.6)	**28.** E (3.1)
5. D (8.1, 2.3)	**17.** C (5.4, 4.3)	**29.** E (4.5, 2.8)
6. E (2.9)	**18.** B (8.1, 4.3)	**30.** A (2.8)
7. C (2.1)	**19.** C (1.7, 2.9)	**31.** C (2.11, 2.9)
8. C (3.5, 2.6, 2.1)	**20.** C (4.2, 2.7)	**32.** E (2.1, 1.6)
9. D (2.1, 2.9, 3.4)	**21.** D (1.5, 1.2)	**33.** D (3.1, 8.1)
10. E (5.4, 2.7)	**22.** C (2.11, 2.1, 1.6)	**34.** E (2.11, 7.6)
11. A (7.6, 7.4, 7.3)	**23.** B (2.11, 1.5, 1.6)	**35.** A (2.3)
12. D (2.8, 2.6, 4.6)	**24.** C (4.4, 2.6)	

Solutions for
SAT-Type Algebra Test 1

1. (E) Solve $\frac{8}{r} = 2$ for r.

$$2r = 8$$
$$r = 4$$

Substitute 4 for r in $3s + r = 19$.

$$3s + 4 = 19$$
$$3s = 15$$
$$s = 5$$

2. (C) In a proportion, the product of the means equals the product of the extremes.

$$\frac{12}{z} = \frac{3}{8}$$
$$(3)(z) = (8)(12)$$
$$3z = 96$$
$$z = 32$$

3. (C) Since the product of two unlike integers is negative, it follows that $(-)(-) = +$ and $(+)(-) = -$.

4. (D) Substitute 3 for x in $y = 2x^2 - 3x$.

$$y = 2(3)^2 - 3(3)$$
$$y = 18 - 9$$
$$y = 9$$

5. (D) Scale I ranges 100° from 0° to 100°. Scale II starts at 50° and ranges 250° from 50° to 300°.

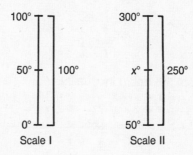

Scale I   Scale II

Write an equation.

Scale II $= \frac{250}{100}$ (Scale I) $+ 50$

Scale II $= \frac{5}{2}$ (Scale I) $+ 50$

Scale II $= \frac{5}{2}$ (50) $+ 50$

Scale II $= 125 + 50$

Scale II $= 175°$

6. (E) Multiply the first equation $x - y = n$ by the second equation $x + y = \frac{1}{n}$.

Thus, $(x - y)(x + y) = n\left(\frac{1}{n}\right)$

$$x^2 - y^2 = 1$$

7. (C) $\quad 2^2 = 2 \cdot 2 = 4$ and $3^2 = 3 \cdot 3 = 9$

$(2 + 3)^2 = 5^2 = 5 \cdot 5 = 25$

Thus, $2^2 + 3^2 + (2 + 3)^2 = 4 + 9 + 25 = 38$.

8. (C) $\qquad \sqrt{9 - 6y + y^2} = \sqrt{(3 - y)^2}$

Substitute 4 for y. $\qquad = \sqrt{(3 - 4)^2}$

$\qquad = \sqrt{(-1)^2}$

$\qquad = \sqrt{1}$

$\qquad = 1$

9. (D) I. $(ab)^2 = a^2b^2$ is true for all integers.

II. $a^2 - b^2$ is the difference of two squares and can be factored into the sum and difference of the square root of each number. $a^2 - b^2 = (a + b)(a - b)$

III. $(a + b)^2 = (a + b)(a + b)$

$\qquad = a^2 + ab + ab + b^2$

$\qquad = a^2 + 2ab + b^2$

Thus, $a^2 + 2ab + b^2 = a^2 + b^2$ only if $2ab = 0$.

Thus, statements I and II are always true.

10. (E) If $\quad \frac{e}{f} = \frac{1}{3}, \qquad$ If $\quad \frac{g}{h} = \frac{1}{6},$

then $3e = f.\qquad\qquad$ then $6g = h.$

Add the two equations.

$$3e + 6g = f + h$$
$$3(e + 2g) = f + h$$
$$\frac{3(e + 2g)}{f + h} = 1$$
$$\frac{e + 2g}{f + h} = \frac{1}{3}$$

11. (A) Subtract 7 from the entire inequality.

$$-1 < \quad 4x + 7 \quad < 11$$
$$-1 - 7 < 4x + 7 - 7 < 11 - 7$$
$$-8 < 4x < 4$$

Divide by 4. $\qquad -2 < x < 1$

12. (D) Add the fractions.

$\qquad \frac{1}{n} - \frac{1}{m} = \frac{m}{mn} - \frac{n}{mn} \qquad\qquad$ LCD $= mn$

$\qquad\qquad = \frac{m - n}{mn}$

Since $n - m = -3$, then $-(n - m) = -(-3)$

$$m - n = 3$$

Thus, $\frac{m - n}{mn} = \frac{3}{3} = 1$.

13. (B) The car travels uphill for 100 miles at 40 mph, so

$$r \times t = d$$
$$40t = 100$$
$$t = 2\frac{1}{2} \text{ hours}$$

It travels downhill for 100 miles at 60 mph, so

$$60t = 100$$
$$t = 1\frac{2}{3} \text{ hours}$$

The total time required to go 100 miles uphill and downhill is

$$2\frac{1}{2} + 1\frac{2}{3} = 2\frac{3}{6} + 1\frac{4}{6}$$
$$= 3\frac{7}{6} = 4\frac{1}{6} \text{ hours}$$

Since the total distance traveled is 200 miles, the average rate is the total distance divided by the total time.

$$r = \frac{d}{t}$$
$$r = \frac{200}{4\frac{1}{6}} = \frac{200}{\frac{25}{6}}$$
$$r = 200 \div \frac{25}{6}$$
$$r = \frac{\overset{8}{\cancel{200}}}{1} \times \frac{6}{\underset{1}{\cancel{25}}}$$
$$r = 48 \text{ mph}$$

14. (C) Add the expressions on the left side of the equation.

$$\frac{1}{p} - \frac{1}{q - 1} = \frac{2}{3}$$

$$\frac{q - 1}{p(q - 1)} - \frac{p}{p(q - 1)} = \frac{2}{3} \qquad \text{LCD} = p(q - 1)$$

$$\frac{q - 1 - p}{pq - p} = \frac{2}{3}$$

Substitute 6 for $pq - p$.

$$\frac{q - p - 1}{6} = \frac{2}{3}$$
$$q - p - 1 = \frac{2}{\cancel{3}} (\cancel{6})^2$$
$$q - p - 1 = 4$$
$$q - p = 5$$

15. (C) If the product of two numbers is zero, then either one of the factors is zero or both factors are zero.

Since $(r - 1)\left(\frac{1}{r}\right) = 0,$

then $r - 1 = 0 \text{ or } \frac{1}{r} = 0 \quad$ (Impossible)

$$r = 1$$

Thus, $r = 1$ is the only possible solution.

16. (E)
$$x^2 + xy - 3x - 3y = 0$$
$$x^2 + xy = 3x + 3y$$
$$x(x + y) = 3(x + y)$$
For x to equal 3, we must exclude the possibility that $x + y = 0$.
To ensure that $x + y \neq 0$, $x \neq -y$.

17. (C) Solve each proportion.

$$\frac{3}{4} = \frac{x}{6} \qquad \frac{6}{y} = \frac{4}{3}$$
$$4x = 18 \qquad 4y = 18$$
$$x = \frac{18}{4} \qquad y = \frac{18}{4}$$

Thus, $x = y$.

18. (B) The sum of 10 and twice some number s is $2s + 10$.
Write the equation and solve.
$$3(2s + 10) = 54$$
$$6s + 30 = 54$$
$$6s = 24$$
$$s = 4$$

19. (C) Use the distributive property to multiply $y^2(y + 1)$.
The product $y^3 + y^2$ is equal to 1.

Thus, the two expressions are equal to each other.

20. (C) Add 1 to both sides of the proportion.

$$\frac{a}{b} = \frac{c}{d}$$
$$\frac{a}{b} + 1 = \frac{c}{d} + 1$$
$$\frac{a}{b} + \frac{b}{b} = \frac{c}{d} + \frac{d}{d}$$
$$\frac{a + b}{b} = \frac{c + d}{d}$$

21. (D) If $y > 0$ and x is any integer, then $x - y$ can be a negative or positive integer as shown below.

If $x = -3$ and $y = 5$, then $-3 - 5 = -8$.
If $x = 0$ and $y = 5$, then $0 - 5 = -5$.
If $x = 8$ and $y = 5$, then $8 - 5 = 3$.

Thus, the relationship cannot be determined.

22. (C) Use the relationship given to evaluate each quantity.
$$N^* = (N - 2)^2$$

If $N = 1$, $1^* = (1 - 2)^2$
$$1^* = (-1)^2 = 1$$

If $N = 3$, $3^* = (3 - 2)^2$
$$3^* = 1^2 = 1$$

23. (B) The value of each expression is found in two steps.

$1 * (2 * 3)$

$2 * 3 = \frac{2(2) - 3}{2(3) - 2} = \frac{4 - 3}{6 - 2}$

$= \frac{1}{4}$

$1 * \frac{1}{4} = \frac{2(1) - \frac{1}{4}}{2\left(\frac{1}{4}\right) - 1}$

$= \frac{2 - \frac{1}{4}}{\frac{1}{2} - 1} = \frac{\frac{7}{4}}{-\frac{1}{2}} = -\frac{7}{2}$

$1 * (2 * 3) = -\frac{7}{2}$

$(1 * 2) * 3$

$1 * 2 = \frac{2(1) - 2}{2(2) - 1} = \frac{2 - 2}{4 - 1}$

$= 0$

$0 * 3 = \frac{2(0) - 3}{2(3) - 0}$

$= \frac{0 - 3}{6 - 0}$

$(1 * 2) * 3 = \frac{-3}{6} = -\frac{1}{2}$

Thus, $-\frac{1}{2} > -\frac{7}{2}$.

24. (C) Substitute -5 for x:

$y = x^2 + 8x + 15$
$y = (-5)^2 + 8(-5) + 15$
$y = 25 - 40 + 15$
$y = 0$

Substitute -3 for x:

$y = x^2 + 8x + 15$
$y = (-3)^2 + 8(-3) + 15$
$y = 9 - 24 + 15$
$y = 0$

25. (A) Choose three values for b and find the corresponding values for a.

If $b = -3$, then $a > -3 + 1$ or $a > -2$ $(-2 > -3)$.
If $b = 0$, then $a > 0 + 1$ or $a > 1$ $(1 > 0)$.
If $b = 2$, then $a > 2 + 1$ or $a > 3$ $(3 > 2)$.

Thus, in each case $a > b$.

26. (C) Since $(p + q)^2 = p^2 + 2pq + q^2$,
then $(p + q)^2 - 2pq = p^2 + 2pq + q^2 - 2pq = p^2 + q^2$.

Thus, $p^2 + q^2 = (p + q)^2 - 2pq$.

27. (D) Since each number is twice the previous one, represent $w, x, y,$ and z as $w, 2w, 4w,$ and $8w$, respectively.

Then test each of the given choices.
(A) $w + 2w + 4w \neq 8w$ False
(B) $w + 4w \overset{?}{=} 2w + 8w$
       $5w \neq 10w$ False
(C) $w(4w) \overset{?}{=} 2w(8w)$
       $4w^2 \neq 16w^2$ False
(D) $\frac{8w}{2w} \overset{?}{=} \frac{4w}{w}$
       $4 = 4$ True
(E) $\frac{w(2w)}{4w} \overset{?}{=} 8w$
       $\frac{w}{2} \neq 8w$ False

28. **(E)** Test each of the given choices. A prime number is, by definition, one that is divisible only by itself and one. Thus, the prime numbers are 2, 3, 5, 7, 11, 13, 17, and so on.

    (A) $3 + 7 = 10$ Not prime
    (B) $2 + 5 = 7$ Not even
    (C) $3 + 5 = 8$ Not odd
    (D) If the numbers are equal, the sum can never be prime since it is always divisible by 2.
    (E) This must be the correct choice. See (D) above.

29. **(E)** Multiply both terms of the fraction by y.

$$\frac{y\left(\frac{x}{y}\right)}{y(y)} = x^2$$

$$\frac{x}{y^2} = x^2$$

$$x = x^2 y^2$$

$$\frac{x}{x^2} = y^2 \quad \text{or} \quad y^2 = \frac{1}{x}$$

$$y = \pm \sqrt{\frac{1}{x}}$$

If $x = \frac{1}{4}$, then $y = \pm 2$.

30. **(A)** The LCD is $x(x + 1)$.
Then,

$$\frac{x}{x + 1} - \frac{x - 1}{x} =$$

$$\frac{x(x)}{x(x + 1)} - \frac{(x + 1)(x - 1)}{x(x + 1)} =$$

$$\frac{x^2 - (x^2 - 1)}{x(x + 1)} =$$

$$\frac{x^2 - x^2 + 1}{x(x + 1)} = \frac{1}{x(x + 1)}$$

If your choice was
(B), you multiplied the terms of the first fraction by $x + 1$ and the second fraction by x.
(C), you used $x + 1$ as the LCD.
(D), you used x as the LCD.
(E), you used the distributive property incorrectly when simplifying $\frac{x^2 - (x^2 - 1)}{x(x + 1)}$.

31. **(C)** If

$$x * y = \frac{x - 2y^3}{y^2}$$

then,

$$10^6 * 10^2 = \frac{10^6 - 2(10^2)^3}{(10^2)^2}$$

$$= \frac{10^6 - 2(10^6)}{10^4}$$

$$= \frac{-1(10^6)}{10^4}$$

$$= -1(10^2) = -10^2$$

If your choice was
(A), you evaluated $(10^2)^3$ as 10^5.
(B), you wrote $10^6 - 2(10^5)$ as $-2(10)$.
(D), you divided $\frac{10^6}{10^4}$ as $\frac{1}{10^2}$.
(E), you forgot to write the negative sign.

0

32. (E) If $z^2 = 2$, then $z = \pm\sqrt{2}$.

$$z^3 = (\sqrt{2})^3 \qquad\qquad z^3 = (-\sqrt{2})^3$$
$$z^3 = (\sqrt{2})(\sqrt{2})(\sqrt{2}) \qquad z^3 = (-\sqrt{2})(-\sqrt{2})(-\sqrt{2})$$
$$z^3 = 2\sqrt{2} \qquad\qquad z^3 = -2\sqrt{2}$$

If your choice was
(A), you evaluated $(-\sqrt{2})^3$ as $-\sqrt{6}$.
(B), you solved $z^2 = 2$ for the positive root $\sqrt{2}$ only.
(C), you solved $z^2 = 2$ for the negative root $-\sqrt{2}$ only.
(D), you evaluated $(\sqrt{2})^3$ as $\sqrt{6}$.

33. (D) The two smallest positive integers divisible by 23 are $23 = 1(23)$ and $46 = 2(23)$. Thus, the smallest possible sum of y and z is $23 + 46$ or 69.

If your choice was
(A), you missed the word *distinct* and then considered 0 as a positive integer.
(B), you used 0 and 23 as two positive integers.
(C), you missed the word *distinct* and found $23 + 23 = 46$.
(E), you skipped 46 and used 23 and 69.

34. (E) If

$$x \,\square\, y = \frac{x}{x-1} - \frac{y+1}{y},$$

then

$$3 \,\square\, 6 = \frac{3}{3-1} - \frac{6+1}{6}$$
$$= \frac{3}{2} - \frac{7}{6}$$
$$= \frac{9}{6} - \frac{7}{6} = \frac{2}{6} \text{ or } \frac{1}{3}$$

Compare this result with the fractions $\frac{1}{4}$ and $\frac{1}{2}$. Thus, $\frac{1}{4} < \frac{1}{3} < \frac{1}{2}$.

If your choice was
(A or B), you misread the compound inequality.
(C or D), see the solution above.

35. (A) The cost at d dollars per day for 12 days is $12d$ dollars. The cost at x cents per mile for 600 miles is $600x$ cents or $\frac{600x}{100} = 6x$ dollars.
Thus, the total cost is $(12d + 6x)$ or $6(2d + x)$ dollars.

If your choice was
(B), you divided both $12d$ dollars and $600x$ cents by 100.
(C), you found the cost in cents.
(D), you forgot to change $600x$ cents to dollars.
(E), you reversed the cost of the rental and the cost of the mileage.

Answer Sheet*

SAT-Type Algebra Test 2

1. (A) (B) (C) (D) (E)
2. (A) (B) (C) (D) (E)
3. (A) (B) (C) (D) (E)
4. (A) (B) (C) (D) (E)
5. (A) (B) (C) (D) (E)
6. (A) (B) (C) (D) (E)
7. (A) (B) (C) (D) (E)
8. (A) (B) (C) (D) (E)
9. (A) (B) (C) (D) (E)
10. (A) (B) (C) (D) (E)
11. (A) (B) (C) (D) (E)
12. (A) (B) (C) (D) (E)
13. (A) (B) (C) (D) (E)
14. (A) (B) (C) (D) (E)
15. (A) (B) (C) (D) (E)
16. (A) (B) (C) (D) (E)
17. (A) (B) (C) (D) (E)
18. (A) (B) (C) (D) (E)

19. (A) (B) (C) (D) (E)
20. (A) (B) (C) (D) (E)
21. (A) (B) (C) (D) (E)
22. (A) (B) (C) (D) (E)
23. (A) (B) (C) (D) (E)
24. (A) (B) (C) (D) (E)
25. (A) (B) (C) (D) (E)
26. (A) (B) (C) (D) (E)
27. (A) (B) (C) (D) (E)
28. (A) (B) (C) (D) (E)
29. (A) (B) (C) (D) (E)
30. (A) (B) (C) (D) (E)
31. (A) (B) (C) (D) (E)
32. (A) (B) (C) (D) (E)
33. (A) (B) (C) (D) (E)
34. (A) (B) (C) (D) (E)
35. (A) (B) (C) (D) (E)

*An Answer Sheet very much like this will be given to you at the actual test. In doing the following practice test, you may wish to record your answers on this Answer Sheet. However, it may be more convenient for you to circle your answer from among the choices provided.

SAT-Type Algebra Test 2

Directions:
Solve each problem in this practice test. Use any available space on the page for scratchwork. Then decide which is the best of the choices given and either darken the corresponding space on the Answer Sheet on page 152 or circle your answer from among the choices provided.

1. If $z - c = z + 4$, then $c =$

(A) -4 (B) 4 (C) $-z$ (D) z (E) $-2z + 4$

2. If $x^2 - 5x - 6 = 0$, then x could be

(A) -3 (B) -2 (C) -1 (D) 1 (E) 2

3. If the sum of $t - 1, t$, and $t + 1$ is 0, then $t =$

(A) $-\frac{2}{3}$ (B) $-\frac{1}{3}$ (C) 0 (D) $\frac{1}{3}$ (E) $\frac{2}{3}$

4. The sum s of the terms of a geometric progression is $s = \frac{rl - a}{r - 1}$, in which the first term is a, the last term is l, and the common ratio is r. What is a when $s = 1020, r = 2$, and $l = 512$?

(A) -4 (B) 4 (C) -2 (D) 2 (E) 508

5. Mario bought ten more 17¢ stamps than 22¢ stamps. He also bought three times as many 2¢ stamps as the number of 17¢ stamps. If the number of 22¢ stamps is x, then an expression for the number of 2¢ stamps, in terms of x, is

(A) $3x$ (B) $x + 10$ (C) $33x$ (D) $3x + 10$ (E) $3x + 30$

6. If x, y, and z are consecutive odd integers and $x < y < z$, then, in terms of z, $x =$

(A) $z + 2$ (B) $z - 1$ (C) $z - 2$ (D) $z - 4$ (E) $z + 4$

7. If $\frac{1}{2} + \frac{1}{3} + \frac{1}{5} = \frac{31}{N}$, then all of the following are integers EXCEPT

(A) $\frac{N}{3}$ (B) $\frac{N}{12}$ (C) $\frac{N}{15}$ (D) $\frac{N}{6}$ (E) $\frac{N}{10}$

8. If $8 - y < 5$ and if y is one of the numbers $-3, 0, 3, 5$, or 9, what is the value of y?

(A) -3 (B) 3 (C) 5 (D) 9
(E) It cannot be determined from the information given.

9. What is the result when $3 - 4x$ is subtracted from the product of $2 + 3x$ and $x - 5$?

(A) $3x^2 - 17x - 7$ (B) $-3x^2 - 17x - 7$ (C) $3x^2 - 9x - 13$
(D) $-3x^2 + 9x + 13$ (E) $3x^2 - 17x - 13$

10. How many arrangements of the letters of the word *problem* are possible with *b* as the middle letter?

(A) 30   (B) 120   (C) 360   (D) 720   (E) 5040

11. If *r* is to *s* as *s* is to *t*, and 3 is to *t* as *r* is to 12, then *s* could be

(A) −6   (B) 3   (C) 12   (D) 18   (E) 36

12. If $3b + 1 = a$, what is the value of $a^2 - 6ab + 9b^2 - 1$?

(A) −2   (B) −1   (C) 0   (D) 1   (E) 2

13. If $(2^3 - 2^2)(2^4 - 2^3) = 2^x$, what is *x*?

(A) 2   (B) 3   (C) 4   (D) 5   (E) 6

14. If $3a - 5b = 12$ and $a = 3b$, then $a =$

(A) −6   (B) 3   (C) 6   (D) 9   (E) 12

15. If *p*, *q*, and *r* are positive integers and $p < q < r$, which of the following statements is (are) always true?

I. $p(qr) = (pq)r$
II. $\frac{p^q}{p^r} = p^{r-q}$
III. $\sqrt{p}\,\sqrt{r} = \sqrt{pr}$

(A) I only   (B) II only   (C) III only
(D) I and II only   (E) I and III only

16. If $a \square b = a^2 - b^2$, what could be a value for *a* so that $a \square 3 = 27$?

(A) −6   (B) $2\sqrt{6}$ (C) 18   (D) 24
(E) It cannot be determined

Questions 17-26 each consist of two quantities, one in Column A and one in Column B. You are to compare the two quantities and on the answer sheet blacken space

A if the quantity in Column A is greater;
B if the quantity in Column B is greater;
C if the two quantities are equal;
D if the relationship cannot be determined
from the information given.

An E response will not be scored.

Notes:
1. In certain questions, information concerning one or both of the quantities to be compared is centered above the two columns.
2. In a given question, a symbol that appears in both columns represents the same thing in Column A as it does in Column B.
3. Letters such as *x*, *n*, and *k* stand for real numbers.

	Column A	*Column B*

$$a = b = c = d = e$$

17. $b + 3c$ | $a + c + d + e$

---

18. The number of prime integers greater than 2 and less than 15 | The number of odd integers greater than 2 and less than 15

$$x > y$$

19. x^2 | y^2

$$p = 8q \text{ and } r = 4s$$

20. $2qr$ | ps

$$0 < x < 1$$

21. x | $\sqrt{\frac{1}{x}}$

---

22. $a^2 - b^2 + 2b(b - a)$ | $(a - b)^2$

---

abc is a negative integer
$$a < 0 \text{ and } b > 0$$

23. c | 0

$$a^2 > 1 + b^2$$

24. 1 | $(a + b)(a - b)$

$$\sqrt{(a - b)^2} = a - b$$
$$a \neq b$$

25. b | a

---

k and x are integers and $k^x = 256$

26. k | x

---

27. At what point (x, y) do the lines $y = 3x + 2$ and $2y - x = -6$ intersect?

    (A) $(-2, -4)$ (B) $(2, -4)$ (C) $(-2, 4)$ (D) $(2, 4)$
    (E) The lines do not intersect.

28. If $-1 \le x \le 1$, and $-3 \le y \le -2$, and $z = (x - y)^2$, the least possible value of z is

    (A) 0
    (B) 1
    (C) 4
    (D) 9
    (E) 16

29. Sharon buys a note pad for $1.15. She has 10 pennies, 10 nickels, 5 dimes, and 4 quarters. If she wants to use as many coins as possible to pay for her purchase without receiving change, how many coins does she use?

    (A) 21 (B) 22 (C) 23 (D) 24 (E) 25

30. If $ab = 1$, and $a^2 - 2ab + b^2 = 10$, then $(a + b)^2 =$

    (A) 3
    (B) 6
    (C) 9
    (D) 10
    (E) 14

31. The children's room at the library has a number of bookshelves with 90 books on each shelf. If 4 new bookshelves are added, each bookshelf will then hold only 50 books. How many books does the children's room hold in all?

    (A) 5 (B) 9 (C) 400
    (D) 450 (E) 500

32. $3\sqrt{18} - \sqrt{48} + \sqrt{75} =$

    (A) $3\sqrt{45}$ (B) $9\sqrt{2} + 1$ (C) $9\sqrt{2} + \sqrt{3}$
    (D) $9\sqrt{2} + 3\sqrt{3}$ (E) $9\sqrt{5}$

33. The ratio of the units digit to the tens digit of a two-digit number is one to two. If the tens digit is two more than the units digit, then the units digit is

(A) 2   (B) 3   (C) 4   (D) 5   (E) 6

34. Some boys want to share the cost of a trip. The cost is C dollars per boy. If x boys drop out, the cost per person goes up y dollars, assuming the total price of the trip remains the same. In terms of $C, x,$ and y, the number of boys initially is

(A) $\dfrac{-xy}{2C}$ (B) $\dfrac{y(C+x)}{x}$ (C) $\dfrac{x(C+y)}{y}$

(D) $\dfrac{-x(C+y)}{y}$ (E) $\dfrac{x(C+y)}{y-2C}$

35. If $p < q < 0$, then which of the following is always true?

  I. $-p < -q$

 II. $p^2 + q^2 > 1$

III. $\dfrac{p}{q} > 1$

(A) I only   (B) II only   (C) III only
(D) I and III only   (E) II and III only

Answer Key to SAT-Type Algebra Test 2

Following each answer, there is a number or numbers in the form *"a.b"* in parentheses. This number refers to the Algebra Refresher Section (beginning on page 23). The first number *"a"* indicates the section:

1. Integers
2. Algebraic Expressions
3. Factoring
4. Equations

5. Ratio and Proportion
6. Probability
7. Inequalities
8. Problem Solving

The number *"b"* indicates the part of the section that explains the rule or method used in solving the problem.

---

1. A (4.2, 1.6)
2. C (4.4, 3.5)
3. C (4.3, 4.2)
4. B (2.6, 4.2)
5. E (2.3)
6. D (8.2, 2.3, 4.2)
7. B (4.2, 2.6, 3.1)
8. E (7.4, 7.3)
9. C (2.9, 2.8, 2.7)
10. D (6.1)
11. A (5.3, 5.4, 4.4)
12. C (4.6, 4.3, 2.9)

13. D (1.7, 2.9)
14. D (4.6, 4.3)
15. E (1.7, 2.10, 2.1)
16. A (2.11, 3.4)
17. C (4.1, 4.2)
18. B (3.1)
19. D (7.1, 2.1)
20. C (2.9)
21. B (7.1, 2.1)
22. C (2.9, 2.8, 3.5)
23. A (1.6, 1.1)
24. B (7.4, 3.4)

25. B (4.3)
26. D (2.1)
27. A (4.6, 4.11)
28. B (7.6, 4.5)
29. D (8.5)
30. E (4.3, 4.5)
31. D (2.3, 8.1, 4.3)
32. C (2.1)
33. A (8.1, 2.3, 4.6)
34. C (8.7, 2.3)
35. C (7.1)

Solutions for SAT-Type Algebra Test 2

1. (A)
$$z - c = z + 4$$
Subtract z from both sides of the equation.
$$z - c - z = z + 4 - z$$
$$-c = 4$$
Multiply both sides by -1.
$$(-1)(-c) = (-1)4$$
$$c = -4$$

2. (C) Factor the expression $x^2 - 5x - 6$ to get $(x - 6)(x + 1) = 0$.
Set each factor equal to 0.
$$x - 6 = 0 \quad \text{or} \quad x + 1 = 0$$
$$x = 6 \qquad\qquad x = -1$$
The answer is $x = 6$ and $x = -1$.

3. (C)
$$(t - 1) + t + (t + 1) = 0$$
$$3t = 0$$
$$t = 0$$

4. (B) Substitute 1020 for s, 2 for r, and 512 for l in
$$s = \frac{rl - a}{r - 1}$$
$$1020 = \frac{2(512) - a}{2 - 1}$$
$$1020 = 1024 - a$$
$$-4 = -a$$
$$a = 4$$

5. (E) Let
$$x = \text{the number of } 22\text{¢ stamps}$$
$$x + 10 = \text{the number of } 17\text{¢ stamps}$$
$$3(x + 10) = \text{the number of } 24\text{¢ stamps}$$

Thus, $3(x + 10) = 3x + 30$.

6. (D) If x, y, and z are consecutive odd integers
with $x < y < z$, then $y = x + 2$ and $z = y + 2$.
Substitute $x + 2$ for y in $z = y + 2$.
$$z = x + 2 + 2$$
$$z = x + 4$$
$$z - 4 = x$$

7. (B) The LCD = 30, so
$$\frac{1}{2} + \frac{1}{3} + \frac{1}{5} = \frac{31}{N}$$
$$\frac{15}{30} + \frac{10}{30} + \frac{6}{30} = \frac{31}{N}$$
$$\frac{31}{30} = \frac{31}{N}$$

Therefore, $N = 30$.

Each choice is an integer if the denominator is a factor of 30. The factors of 30 are 1, 2, 3, 5, 6, 10, 15, 30.
Thus, $\frac{n}{12}$ is *not* an integer.

8. **(E)** Add y to both sides of the inequality.
$$8 - y < 5$$
$$8 < 5 + y$$
Subtract 5 from both sides of the inequality.
$$3 < y \quad \text{or} \quad y > 3$$
Therefore, y could be 5 or 9 and cannot be determined.

9. **(C)** Use the distributive property to find the product of $2 + 3x$ and $x - 5$.
$$(2 + 3x)(x - 5) = (2 + 3x)x + (2 + 3x)(-5)$$
$$= 2x + 3x^2 - 10 - 15x$$
$$= 3x^2 - 13x - 10$$
Then, $(3x^2 - 13x - 10) - (3 - 4x) =$
$$3x^2 - 13x - 10 - 3 + 4x = 3x^2 - 9x - 13$$

10. **(D)** A middle letter of b can occur in only one way.

			b			

The first letter can be any of 6 possible letters, 5 for the second letter, 4 for the third letter, 1 for the middle letter, 3 for the fifth letter, 2 for the sixth letter, and 1 for the seventh letter.

6	5	4	1	3	2	1

Thus, there are $6 \cdot 5 \cdot 4 \cdot 1 \cdot 3 \cdot 2 \cdot 1$ or 720 possible arrangements.

11. **(A)** Write the proportions and solve.

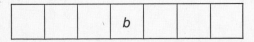

$$\frac{r}{s} = \frac{s}{t} \qquad\qquad \frac{3}{t} = \frac{r}{12}$$
$$s^2 = rt \qquad\qquad rt = 36$$

$$s^2 = 36$$
$$s^2 - 36 = 0$$
$$(s + 6)(s - 6) = 0$$
$$s + 6 = 0 \quad \text{or} \quad s - 6 = 0$$
$$s = -6 \qquad\qquad s = 6$$

Thus, s could be -6.

12. **(C)** Substitute $3b + 1$ for a.
$$a^2 - 6ab + 9b^2 - 1 = (3b + 1)^2 - 6(3b + 1)b + 9b^2 - 1$$
$$= 9b^2 + 6b + 1 - 18b^2 - 6b + 9b^2 - 1$$
$$= 18b^2 - 18b^2 + 6b - 6b + 1 - 1$$
$$= 0$$

13. (D) Use the distributive property to multiply $2^3 - 2^2$ and $2^4 - 2^3$.

$$(2^3 - 2^2)(2^4 - 2^3) = 2^x$$
$$(2^3 - 2^2)\,2^4 + (2^3 - 2^2)(-2^3) = 2^x$$
$$2^7 - 2^6 - 2^6 + 2^5 = 2^x$$
$$2^7 - 2(2^6) + 2^5 = 2^x$$
$$2^7 - 2^7 + 2^5 = 2^x$$
$$2^5 = 2^x$$

Therefore, $x = 5$.

14. (D) Substitute $3b$ for a in $3a - 5b = 12$.

$$3(3b) - 5b = 12$$
$$9b - 5b = 12$$
$$4b = 12$$
$$b = 3$$

If $a = 3b$, then $a = 3(3) = 9$.

15. (E) I is the associative property of multiplication and is always true.
II is not true since the law of exponents for division states that $\frac{p^q}{p^r} = p^{q-r}$.

III is always true for positive integers. For example, $\sqrt{9}\,\sqrt{4} = \sqrt{36}$ since $3 \cdot 2 = 6$.

16. (A) If $a \,\square\, b = a^2 - b^2$, then $a \,\square\, 3 = a^2 - 3^2 = a^2 - 9$.
Since $a \,\square\, 3 = 27$, then $a^2 - 9 = 27$

$$a^2 = 36$$
$$a^2 - 36 = 0$$
$$(a + 6)(a - 6) = 0$$
$$a + 6 = 0 \quad \text{or} \quad a - 6 = 0$$
$$a = -6 \qquad\qquad a = 6$$

17. (C) If $a = b = c = d = e$, then $b + 3c = b + 3b = 4b$.
$a + c + d + e = b + b + b + b = 4b$

Thus, the two expressions are equal to each other.

18. (B) The five prime integers greater than 2 and less than 15 are 3, 5, 7, 11, and 13. The six odd integers greater than 2 and less than 15 are 3, 5, 7, 9, 11, and 13.

19. (D) For all positive integers, if $x > y$, then $x^2 > y^2$.
For all negative integers, if $x > y$, then $x^2 < y^2$.

Thus, the relationship cannot be determined from the information given.

20. (C) If $p = 8q$, then $8q = p$.
Multiply $8q = p$ by $r = 4s$.

Thus, $8qr = 4ps$
$2qr = ps$

21. (B) Test each expression for some values of x such that $0 < x < 1$.

If $x = \frac{1}{4}$, then $\sqrt{\dfrac{1}{\frac{1}{4}}} = \sqrt{4} = 2$.

If $x = \frac{1}{9}$, then $\sqrt{\dfrac{1}{\frac{1}{9}}} = \sqrt{9} = 3$.

If $x = \frac{1}{16}$, then $\sqrt{\dfrac{1}{\frac{1}{16}}} = \sqrt{16} = 4$.

Thus, $\sqrt{\dfrac{1}{x}} > x$ for $0 < x < 1$.

22. (C)
$$a^2 - b^2 + 2b(b - a) = a^2 - b^2 + 2b^2 - 2ab$$
$$= a^2 + b^2 - 2ab$$
$$= a^2 - 2ab + b^2$$
$$= (a - b)^2$$

23. (A) For abc to be negative, an odd number of integers must be negative. Since a is negative ($a < 0$) and b is positive ($b > 0$), c must also be positive ($c > 0$).

24. (B)
$$a^2 > 1 + b^2$$
Subtract b^2 from both sides of the inequality.
$$a^2 - b^2 > 1 + b^2 - b^2$$
$$a^2 - b^2 > 1$$
Factor the expression $a^2 - b^2$.
$$(a + b)(a - b) > 1$$

25. (B) $\sqrt{x^2} = x$ only if x is not negative.
If x is negative, then $\sqrt{x^2} = -x$.
Since $\sqrt{(a - b)^2} = a - b$, then $a - b$ is not negative and a is greater than or equal to b. Since $a \neq b$, then $a > b$.

26. (D) Since $k^x = 256$, then $k^x = 2^8$ $\quad (k < x)$
$$k^x = 4^4 \quad (k = x)$$
$$k^x = 16^2 \quad (k > x)$$
Therefore, the relationship cannot be determined from the information given.

27. (A) Solve the pair of equations simultaneously.
Substitute $3x + 2$ for y in the equation $2y - x = -6$.
$$2y - x = -6$$
$$2(3x + 2) - x = -6$$
$$6x + 4 - x = -6$$
$$5x = -10$$
$$x = -2$$

Substitute -2 for x in $y = 3x + 2$.
$$y = 3(-2) + 2$$
$$y = -6 + 2$$
$$y = -4$$

The lines intersect at the point $(-2, -4)$.

28. (B) The least possible value of z will occur when x and y are closest to each other. The values of x and y which are closest to each other are $x = -1$ and $y = -2$.
Therefore,
$$z = (x - y)^2$$
$$z = [-1 - (-2)]^2$$
$$z = (-1 + 2)^2$$
$$z = 1^2 \text{ or } 1$$

29. (D) Sharon has a total of
$$10(1) + 10(5) + 5(10) + 4(25)$$
$$10 + 50 + 50 + 100 = 210 \text{ cents or } \$2.10$$

Thus, she will be left with $\$2.10 - \$1.15$ or $\$.95$ after she pays for the object. If she wants to use as many coins as possible, she will be left with the fewest coins. The fewest coins that total $\$.95$, chosen from the coins she has, are 3 quarters and 2 dimes.
Therefore, she will pay for the object with 10 pennies, 10 nickels, 3 dimes, and 1 quarter.
$$10(1) + 10(5) + 3(10) + 1(25) = 10 + 50 + 30 + 25$$
$$= 115 \text{ or } \$1.15$$
Thus, $10 + 10 + 3 + 1 = 24$ coins.

30. (E) Since $a^2 - 2ab + b^2 = 10$, add $4ab$ to both sides of the equation.
$$a^2 - 2ab + b^2 + 4ab = 10 + 4ab$$
$$a^2 + 2ab + b^2 = 10 + 4ab$$
$$(a + b)^2 = 10 + 4ab$$
Substitute 1 for ab.
$$(a + b)^2 = 10 + 4(1)$$
$$(a + b)^2 = 14$$

31. (D) Let $n =$ the number of bookshelves. Then $90n$ represents the total number of books in the children's room. After adding 4 new bookshelves, there were $n + 4$ bookshelves. Each bookshelf now holds 50 books. Since the number of books remains the same, write and solve an equation.
$$90n = 50(n + 4)$$
$$90n = 50n + 200$$
$$40n = 200$$
$$n = 5$$
There were 5 bookshelves originally with 90 books on each shelf, or 450 books in all.

If your choice was
(A), you found the original number of bookshelves.
(B), you found the number of bookshelves after 4 were
added.
(C or E), see the solution above.

32. (C) $3\sqrt{18} = 3\sqrt{9 \cdot 2} = 3\sqrt{9}\sqrt{2} = 3 \cdot 3\sqrt{2} = 9\sqrt{2}$
$-\sqrt{48} = -\sqrt{16 \cdot 3} = -\sqrt{16}\sqrt{3} = -4\sqrt{3}$
$\sqrt{75} = \sqrt{25 \cdot 3} = \sqrt{25}\sqrt{3} = 5\sqrt{3}$
Therefore, $9\sqrt{2} - 4\sqrt{3} + 5\sqrt{3} = 9\sqrt{2} + \sqrt{3}$.

If your choice was
(A), you combined the radicals.
(B), you subtracted the coefficients $(-4, 5)$ and the radicals
$(-\sqrt{3}, \sqrt{3})$ separately.
(D), you evaluated $-\sqrt{16}\sqrt{3}$ as $-\sqrt{4}\sqrt{3} = -2\sqrt{3}$.
(E), you combined the radicals $\sqrt{2}$ and $\sqrt{3}$ as $\sqrt{5}$.

33. (A) Let u = the units digit
t = the tens digit

Then, $\qquad\qquad \dfrac{u}{t} = \dfrac{1}{2}$ or $t = 2u$
$t = u + 2$

Substitute $2u$ for t.
$2u = u + 2$
$u = 2$

If your choice was
(B, D, or E), see the solution above.
(C), you found the value of the tens digit.

34. (C) Let n = the number of boys initially
P = the price of the trip
Then, $\qquad\qquad nC = P$
$(n - x)(C + y) = P$
Therefore, $\qquad (n - x)(C + y) = nC$
$nC + ny - xC - xy = nC$
$ny = xC + xy$
$n = \dfrac{x(C + y)}{y}$

If your choice was
(A), you found the product of $(n - x)(C + y)$ as $nC - xy$ and
then solved $nC = nC - xy$ by subtracting nC from the
right side and adding nC to the left side.
(B), you subtracted y from n and added x to C.
(D), you solved $0 = ny - xC - xy$ as $ny = -xC - xy$.
(E), you added nC to the right side of the equation,
subtracted nC from the left side, and solved
$ny - xC - xy = 2nC$.

35. (C) I is false. If $p < q < 0$, then $-p > -q > 0$.

For example, if $-4 < -3 < 0$, then $+4 > +3 > 0$.

II is false if $p < q < 0$. Try $p = -\frac{1}{2}$ and $q = -\frac{1}{4}$.

Then
$$p^2 + q^2 \overset{?}{>} 1$$
$$\left(-\tfrac{1}{2}\right)^2 + \left(-\tfrac{1}{4}\right)^2 \overset{?}{>} 1$$
$$\tfrac{1}{4} + \tfrac{1}{16} \overset{?}{>} 1$$
$$\tfrac{5}{16} \not> 1$$

III is true. If $p < q < 0$, then $-p > -q$.

Divide by the positive quantity $-q$.
$$-p > -q$$
$$\frac{-p}{-q} > \frac{-q}{-q}$$
$$\frac{p}{q} > 1$$

Try $p = -5$ and $q = -2$.
$$-5 < -2 < 0 \text{ and } 5 > 2$$

Divide by 2.
$$\frac{5}{2} > \frac{2}{2}$$
$$\frac{5}{2} > 1 \quad \text{True}$$

If your choice was
(A, B, D, or E), see the solution above.